TIMEF

HORSES TO FOLLOW

2022 FLAT SEASON

CONTENTS

TIMEFORM

ISBN 978-1-8380349-3-1 Price £10.95

Printed and bound by
Charlesworth Press,
Wakefield, UK 01924 204830

SECTION 1

Timeform's Fifty To Follow, carefully chosen by members of Timeform's editorial staff, are listed below with their respective page numbers. A selection of ten (**marked in bold with a ★**) is made for those who prefer a smaller list.

The form summary for each horse is shown after its age, colour, sex and pedigree. The summary shows the distance, the state of the going and where the horse finished in each of its races on the Flat during 2021. Performances are in chronological sequence with the date of its last race shown at the end.
The distance of each race is given in furlongs, fractional distances being expressed in the decimal notation to the nearest tenth of a furlong. Races run in Britain on all-weather surfaces are prefixed by 'f' for fibresand, 'p' for polytrack and 't' for tapeta.
The going is symbolised as follows: f=firm (turf) or fast (all-weather), m=good to firm (turf) or standard to fast (all-weather); g=good (turf) or standard (all-weather), d=good to soft/dead (turf) or standard to slow (all-weather); s=soft (turf) or slow (all-weather); v=heavy.
Placings are indicated, up to the sixth place, by use of superior figures, an asterisk being used to denote a win.
The Timeform Rating of a horse is simply the merit of the horse expressed in pounds and is arrived at by careful examination of its running against other horses. The ratings range from 130+ for tip-top performers down to a figure of around 20 for the poorest. Symbols attached to the ratings: 'p'–likely to improve; 'P'–capable of much better form; '+'–the horse may be better than we have rated it.

Aldaary 124

4 ch.g. Territories (Ire) – Broughtons Revival (Pivotal)
2021 7d* 7s^3 7f^5 7f^5 7.9m 7s* 8d* Oct 16

Champions Day crowned an excellent unbeaten campaign for Baaeed, who made it six out of six when defeating top older miler Palace Pier in the Queen Elizabeth II Stakes. But he wasn't the only top miling prospect on the Ascot card for trainer William Haggas, jockey Jim Crowley and owner Shadwell. One of only a couple of three-year-olds in the field of 20, progressive stablemate Aldaary won the concluding Balmoral Handicap in the manner of one destined for pattern races himself in 2022. In running to a Timeform rating of 124, he put up one of the best performances seen in a Flat handicap in the last decade, one which in theory would have been good enough to secure him third place behind his stablemate in the QEII.

Aldaary ran out a most impressive winner of the Balmoral, too. Travelling with notable ease in the far-side group, Aldaary produced an immediate response when Crowley asked for his effort, leading over a furlong out and keeping going well to beat Symbolize by a length and a half in a time that was only a fraction slower than Baaeed's earlier on the card. If he does go on to emulate his stablemate in the highest grade, Aldaary wouldn't be the first Balmoral winner to do so. 2017 winner Lord Glitters won the Queen Anne Stakes two years later, while the likes of Lord North, Glen Shiel, Accidental Agent and Here Comes When were all beaten in the Balmoral but went on to become Group 1 winners, too.

Aldaary puts his rivals to the sword in the Balmoral Handicap

Aldaary was a regular at Ascot all season, running there five times in all, with the Balmoral his third win at the track. He already looked a potential group horse when winning a three-year-old handicap over seven furlongs on his reappearance in May and, a fortnight before the Balmoral, inflicted another defeat on Symbolize in the Challenge Cup over the same trip. Under firmer conditions in the summer, Aldaary finished fifth in a couple of Ascot's other valuable seven-furlong handicaps, the Buckingham Palace at the Royal meeting and the International Stakes on King George day.

The well-made Aldaary, who has had a breathing operation and wore a tongue tie at Royal Ascot, stays a mile though the Balmoral was only his second start at the trip and he has the speed for seven furlongs. While he has form under firmer conditions, all his wins have come on ground softer than good. Keeping Aldaary and Baaeed apart will be a nice problem for their trainer to have, though where Aldaary's concerned he's got options in lesser pattern races and will be well up to winning some of those if need be before tackling Group 1 company. ***William Haggas***

Conclusion: ***Lightly raced sort who reached a very smart level last season and should have even more to offer as a four-year-old, representing a yard that has excelled with similar types in the past***

Anmaat (Ire) 111

4 b.g. Awtaad (Ire) – African Moonlight (UAE) (Halling (USA))
2021 p8g* 8m^3 10d^2 10.2m* 10.2f* 9m^2 Sep 25

The downsizing of the Shadwell operation following the death of founder Sheikh Hamdan Al Maktoum last year will impact many trainers in Britain and Ireland in 2022, but none more than Owen Burrows. After all, he had previously trained in a private capacity for the operation at its Kingwood House Stables in Lambourn, his string topping 100 horses at its peak. Now he has moved to the nearby Farncombe Down Stables, a much smaller base and currently home to only 30 or so horses. Forced to reinvent himself as a public trainer, looking for owners, Burrows can at least count some big talents in the Shadwell colours amongst those still in his care for 2022, and the likes of Hukum, Minzaal and Anmaat could prove fine advertisements for his training talents this spring.

Anmaat hasn't established himself in pattern company like Hukum and Minzaal, but he progressed at a rate of knots in 2021, winning handicaps at Bath and Doncaster before signing off with a fine effort in defeat in the Cambridgeshire at Newmarket, going like one still ahead of his mark for a long way. That was his first appearance in a big-field handicap and it seemed to bring out the best in him as he travelled strongly in midfield before being produced to lead approaching the furlong pole. He was only cut down late by Bedouin's Story, ultimately passing the post three quarters of a length behind that rival with another length and a half back to Ametist in third.

A 140,000-guineas purchase as a foal, Anmaat only saw the racecourse once at two, belying market weakness as he shaped with plenty of promise at Kempton, before reappearing to win a novice event at Lingfield in May. From there everything about him was progressive and he remains relatively unexposed, so it will be a surprise if he doesn't pick up a high-end handicap or two this season, with the Lincoln at Doncaster appealing as an obvious target in the spring. A winner over trips ranging from a mile to a mile and a quarter, the strong-travelling Anmaat will have plenty of options beyond

Anmaat (right) ran a cracker when second in the Cambridgeshire

that and he should be able to make a headline or two to aid Burrows' cause in a pivotal year for the trainer. ***Owen Burrows***

Conclusion: *Progressive young handicapper last term and appeals as the sort to win a valuable prize or two this season with more improvement likely*

Aramaic (Ire) 102p

4 b.or br.g. Le Havre (Ire) – Middle Persia (Dalakhani (Ire))
2021 p8s^2 8.9g* 10.3g* 10g^4 Sep 18

William Haggas has few peers when it comes to improving horses through the handicap ranks and he has an interesting project on his hands for 2022 in Aramaic. Strong in the betting but ultimately well beaten on his only start at two, Aramaic proved to be a totally different proposition as a three-year-old, even though his reappearance was delayed until August. When it came it was at Kempton, in a novice event over a mile. The promise of the Newmarket gallops was brought to the track this time and he almost wore down Godolphin hotpot Mo'Assess close home, going down by a neck.

Aramaic opened his account on his next start in a maiden at Musselburgh for which he was sent off the 3/1-on favourite. He still looked a little rough around the edges, but it mattered little given the limitations of his rivals and he barely needed to come off the bridle to beat Hipsway by three and a quarter lengths. A couple of weeks later on his handicap debut at York, Aramaic was much more like the finished article and he proved some way ahead of the assessor stepped up to a mile and a quarter for the first time. He travelled strongly and quickly drew clear after being produced to lead two furlongs out, beating the useful yardstick Pivoine by three and a quarter lengths.

It was no surprise to see Aramaic turned out again quickly, from a revised rating of 94, in the ultra-competitive Dubai Duty Free Handicap at Newbury. He was sent off the 5/2 favourite, but it just didn't happen for him on the day, staying on at the one pace from the two-furlong marker to finish fourth, three and a quarter lengths behind the winner and fellow *Fifty* member Injazati. Aramaic starts the new campaign from the same mark and looks the sort to relish a step up to a mile and a half. A 200,000-guineas yearling, he is by Le Havre and a half-brother to a couple of useful middle-distance performers in Kilimanjaro and Mawaany. Considering his three-year-old campaign was condensed into six weeks, there should be plenty more to come from Aramaic and he is certainly in the right hands to fulfil his undoubted potential. ***William Haggas***

Conclusion: *Made great strides in a short space of time at three and looks the sort to thrive and improve again over middle-distances at four*

Bay Bridge 119p

4 b.c. New Bay – Hayyona (Multiplex)
2021 t10.2s* 10s* 10.3s* 10g* Oct 30

Where would Horses To Follow be without an unexposed Sir Michael Stoute-trained four-year-old on the brink of graduating to pattern company? Many have fitted that description in these pages over the years and Bay Bridge looks another likely type to add to his trainer's well-founded reputation for bringing about further improvement from his older horses. Bay Bridge has had only six races to date, with his three-year-old campaign interrupted by a five-month absence after a foot abscess caused him to miss Royal Ascot. The fact that Bay Bridge held an entry in the King Edward VII Stakes at Ascot suggests that connections have believed they've had a potential group horse on their hands for some time now, and while he didn't get to prove it at three, it could well be a different story in 2022.

Royal Ascot looked very much on the cards after Bay Bridge made it two from two for the year in the London Gold Cup, a three-year-old handicap at Newbury's Lockinge meeting in May which has regularly gone to progressive types destined for better things in recent seasons. Among them was Stoute's 2014 winner Cannock Chase, who won what is now the Hampton Court Stakes at Royal Ascot on his next start before achieving Grade 1 success in Canada as a four-year-old. Bay Bridge was strong in the betting for his handicap debut at Newbury and showed much improved form to win by four lengths after quickening into the lead with two furlongs to run. After showing some promise on a couple of starts late on as a two-year-old, Bay Bridge had made an impressive reappearance on the tapeta at Newcastle, winning a novice by five lengths.

Bay Bridge's Newbury success earned him a 15 lb rise in the weights, but he proved equal to the task when returning in the autumn against some older rivals at York. He had a bit more in hand, too, than the half a length by which he beat the in-form six-year-old Platinumcard. It was that performance, more than any other, which labelled Bay Bridge as one to follow as a four-year-old. He rounded off an unbeaten campaign when stepping up to listed company in the James Seymour Stakes at Newmarket later in October. He had to work harder for his half-length margin of victory this time after eventual runner-up Majestic Dawn raced in a clear lead before Bay Bridge reeled him in late on. The lengthy Bay Bridge, who is likely to stay a mile and a half and acts on soft ground, could have an ideal starting point for his four-year-old campaign in the Gordon Richards Stakes at Sandown, a race his trainer has won 10 times already. ***Sir Michael Stoute***

Conclusion: *Lightly-raced colt whose unbeaten three-year-old campaign promises plenty for his future in middle-distance contests at pattern level like so many before him from the same stable*

Blackrod 104

4 b.c. Mayson – Hilldale (Exceed And Excel (Aus))
2021 6d 6m^2 6m* 5g* 6g^3 Sep 18

Michael Dods is well known for his prowess with sprinters, with dual Nunthorpe winner Mecca's Angel and Prix de l'Abbaye winner Mabs Cross perhaps the two most significant cases in point, and last season he was represented with distinction by Commanche Falls, who registered his fourth handicap success of 2021 when coming out on top in the Stewards' Cup at Goodwood. Dods is a master at getting horses to progress with age—Mecca's Angel and Mabs Cross both produced their peak ratings as five-year-olds—and hopes are high that Blackrod will be the latest sprinter from his yard to climb the ranks.

As a two-year-old Blackrod got off the mark at the second attempt at Hamilton before finding the listed Rockingham Stakes at York a little too hot to handle at that stage of his career. Blackrod shaped as if needing the run on his handicap debut/reappearance at Haydock in May, fading inside the final furlong, and he duly left that effort behind when tackling a valuable handicap at York the following month, as competitive a race as you'll find at that time of the year for three-year-old sprinters. He nearly won it, too, despite being forced to switch over a furlong out, picking up well late on to fill the runner-up spot behind First Folio, beaten a length and a quarter.

Dods decided to follow the traditional route after that defeat, heading to another valuable three-year-old sprint handicap at Newmarket's July Meeting, and this time the verdict went Blackrod's way. Silvestre de Sousa was in the saddle and his partner stayed on strongly in the closing stages to beat Apollo One by a neck. At that stage a step up in trip to seven furlongs looked an attractive option, but instead connections opted to drop back to the minimum trip for the valuable Sky Bet Apprentice Handicap at the Ebor Festival. Blackrod overcame the speed test well, predictably doing all his best work close home to get the better of Digital in another driving finish.

Blackrod was able to race from the same BHA mark of 91 on his final start, when taking on older horses for the first time in the Ayr Silver Cup. A well-backed 9/2 favourite, he couldn't justify that support but shaped as if still in form, doing well under the circumstances to be beaten just a length and three quarters into third after stumbling at the start (also lost a shoe). Still relatively lightly raced, Blackrod is likely to be a fixture in the big sprint handicaps in 2022 and beyond, hopefully winning one or two along the way. He will certainly have plenty of options, effective at both five and six furlongs and likely to stay seven when the situation demands it, too. ***Michael Dods***

Conclusion: *Made rapid strides at three and a BHA mark of 95 still looks workable with a view to the big sprint handicaps in 2022*

Blind Beggar (Ire) 92

4 b.g. Equiano (Fr) – Beylerbey (USA) (Street Cry (Ire))

2021 t5s6 6d2 6v* 6m6 6m 6g3 5g4 6g2 Sep 28

It might seem strange to suggest that there is still a sense of unfinished business with Blind Beggar, at least at first glance. After all, he ran eight times in his three-year-old season and still had just one win in a Catterick maiden (sent-off the 15/8-on favourite and duly scored as he liked by nine lengths) to show for his troubles come the end of the campaign. The bare facts don't tell the whole story, however, and he is still a young horse from whom the best is hopefully still to come.

After getting off the mark at Catterick in May, Blind Beggar failed to make an impact in a couple of valuable three-year-old handicaps at York (beaten three and a half lengths into sixth behind First Folio) and Newmarket (beaten four and a quarter lengths into tenth behind fellow *Fifty* member Blackrod), but he bounced back to form when tackling a field of seasoned sprinters in the Sky Bet Dash back on the Knavesmire. Franny Norton took the ride and Blind Beggar was the subject of a sizeable gamble, being backed down into 4/1 favouritism. For much of the contest he looked like justifying the support, blazing a trail which had most of his rivals out of their comfort zone soon after halfway and only folding late on as Venturous and Music Society came past to fight out the finish. He still had enough left to edge the battle for third, passing the post a length and three quarters behind the winner.

Blind Beggar was then returned to York for the Sky Bet Apprentice Handicap, run over the minimum trip on the final day of the Ebor Festival, and he ran respectably whilst shaping as though probably better at six furlongs than five. Ridden with more restraint on rain-softened ground, he stayed on inside the final furlong to finish fourth behind Blackrod. Typically for one from his yard, Blind Beggar headed next to the Ayr Western Meeting, where he again ran well but was done no favours by the draw on what proved to be his final start. Faring comfortably best of those drawn low, he travelled as well as anything before being left behind by the impressive Big Les inside the final furlong. Blind Beggar will resume from the same BHA mark of 82 in 2022 and there are surely more races to be won with him when everything falls right. Effective on both good to firm and heavy going, he will certainly have plenty of options for his shrewd yard. ***Richard Fahey***

Conclusion: *Highly tried as a three-year-old and should be placed to advantage in lesser sprint handicaps in the North before climbing the ranks*

Boundless Power (Ire) 108

5 br.g. Slade Power (Ire) – Boundless Joy (Aus) (Montjeu (Ire))
2021 p6s^2 5v* 5v^2 5v* 5m^5 6v 5.1m^4 5.6d^2 5s* 5v* Oct 23

Mick Appleby broke through a couple of significant statistical barriers in 2021. For the second time in three years his Rutland yard topped the £1-million mark in domestic earnings, while numerically it was Appleby's best season yet. Passing the milestone of a century of winners for the year with a bit to spare—109 was the final score—was no doubt all the sweeter after coming agonisingly close in the previous two campaigns with a total of 99 winners in both 2019 and 2020. Important contributions to the stable's stats came from progressive sprinter Boundless Power and he could well be playing a significant role again in 2022.

Although placed more often than not in his early days in Ireland, Boundless Power was still a maiden when making his first start for Appleby at Chelmsford in April, but he soon got off the mark in good style in a handicap at Nottingham the following month and quickly added a second success at the same track a few weeks later. He continued to thrive but, as can be the way with sprint handicaps, fortune wasn't always in his favour, notably in the consolation race for the Stewards' Cup at Goodwood over six furlongs (he's almost certainly better at five) and on his next start after that at Windsor where he again met trouble in running but was still beaten only a length or so into fourth.

Boundless Power finally got a fairer crack at things in the Portland at Doncaster in September where his half-length second to another progressive four-year-old, Hurricane Ivor, hinted that he was threatening to come good again before long. Back on softer ground, he duly won his two remaining starts the following month. His third win of the campaign came in a less competitive contest at Ascot, where he justified favouritism by three quarters of a length from Rebel At Dawn, and he showed further improvement back at Doncaster three weeks later. This time Boundless Power had to share the spoils with Tim Easterby's smart Copper Knight, better known for his wins up the road at York, but Boundless Power really caught the eye with how strongly he travelled for much of the contest, leading on the bridle around a furlong out but then digging deep when challenged as the pair of them pulled clear.

On that evidence, Boundless Power was clearly still improving and it won't be a surprise if he can take the step into listed company at least this year. While all of the strong-travelling Boundless Power's wins have come in testing conditions, he didn't run badly on the two occasions he encountered firmer ground in 2021, including for that luckless run at Windsor. ***Michael Appleby***

Conclusion: *Made giant strides in sprint handicaps in his first season with Mick Appleby and no reason to think his progress has finished just yet judging from the way he ended the year*

Dark Shift 101

4 gr.c. Dark Angel (Ire) – Mosuo (Ire) (Oasis Dream)
2021 6.1v* 6m[8] 6g[4] 7v[6] 7m* 8d* Oct 1

It was the proceeds from a gamble on the 1968 Lincoln winner Frankincense which enabled Barry Hills to launch his training career, hence the title of his biography Frankincense And More. Hills went on to train the winner of the Lincoln himself in 2003, Pablo, with one of his sons Michael in the saddle, and now another son Charlie could have a contender for the first big Flat handicap of the turf season. Dark Shift makes his second appearance in Horses To Follow after a successful and profitable three-year-old campaign which saw him win three times, with his last two victories in the autumn coming at odds of 100/30 and 9/2.

Hopefully, Dark Shift can deliver more of the same this year. It was an impressive debut win at Ascot as a two-year-old which prompted his inclusion in last year's book, and he landed the odds in a six-furlong novice at Nottingham on his reappearance last May. After Nottingham, he caught the eye on his handicap debut when mid-division in York's valuable six-furlong handicap for three-year-olds in mid-June, making late headway after a slow start effectively cost him all chance. Having come down the handicap a little, it was three starts later before Dark Shift was back in the winner's enclosure after success in a seven-furlong contest at Ascot. Ryan Moore was in the saddle for the first time and Dark Shift impressed with a surge which took him from the rear to the front of the field, leading in the final 50 yards and well on top at the line as he beat Papacito by three quarters of a length.

That was a useful effort, and one Dark Shift repeated the following month, this time over Ascot's straight mile. With a dozen runners, most of them useful, it looked a strong contest for a classified stakes and it proved every bit as competitive as it looked on paper, with four horses in line well inside the final furlong. Slowly away again, Dark Shift travelled smoothly in rear and once again picked up really well when asked for his effort, this time under Danny Tudhope, coming through deep inside the final furlong to get the better of Bonneval and Walhaan by a head and a neck. That's three wins from four starts at Ascot for Dark Shift, something to bear in mind in any return visits there regardless of how he fares if contesting the Lincoln. He's versatile in terms of ground, having won on both good to firm and heavy. ***Charlie Hills***

Conclusion: *Came from off the pace to end his three-year-old season with a couple of useful wins at Ascot and looks the type to pick up a good mile handicap this year*

Desert Crown 99P

3 b.c. Nathaniel (Ire) – Desert Berry (Green Desert (USA))
2021 8.3s* Nov 3

Owner Saeed Suhail had his blue and yellow colours carried to victory in the 2003 Derby by Kris Kin, described by his trainer Sir Michael Stoute as one of the laziest horses he had handled. The fact that Kris Kin showed so little at home prompted Kieren Fallon, who rode him for the first time at Epsom, to pass him over when he won his Derby trial, the Dee Stakes at Chester as the 20/1 outsider of four, and his lack of sparkle on the gallops also meant his name was missing at the Derby acceptance stage. Fortunately for connections, Kris Kin's Chester win prompted them to come up with the £90,000 fee to add him to the Derby field at the late supplementary stage.

Stoute and Suhail might have another Derby contender on their hands with Desert Crown. It took Kris Kin two goes to win his maiden late in the year as a two-year-old, but Desert Crown went one better, winning first time up at Nottingham in early-November at odds of 11/1. The Stoute two-year-olds are not known for being ready to win on their debuts and he was only of only three such winners in 2021, one of the others sent off at 25/1. Desert Crown could hardly have made a better impression, travelling fluently close to the pace and then storming clear when Richard Kingscote produced him to lead a furlong out to win by five and a half lengths from Schmilsson. The timefigure added substance to the performance, with Desert Crown winning in a time more than two seconds quicker than the winner of the other division of the maiden.

Desert Crown is a half-brother to four winners who, despite all being by the same sire—Archipenko—have won over a variety of trips, including the year-older Cu Chulainn, successful at 11 furlongs last season. His lightly-raced dam won at a mile but with Nathaniel as his sire stamina shouldn't be a worry for Desert Crown at three. The first name that comes to mind with Nathaniel as a sire is, of course, Enable. Rightly so, as she stands out among his offspring on ratings, though curiously all five of Nathaniel's Group or Grade 1 winners to date have been fillies, including last season's Nassau Stakes winner Lady Bowthorpe. Maybe Desert Crown will be the one to redress the balance somewhat and provide him a high-class son. ***Sir Michael Stoute***

Conclusion: *Rare two-year-old to win first time out for his trainer and could hardly have won in better style so one to look out for in a Derby trial with plenty of improvement to come*

Discretion 64p

3 b.f. Dubawi (Ire) – Momentary (Nayef (USA))

2021 8s[5] Sep 30

The Royal colours were carried to victory 36 times in Britain during 2021, making it comfortably the Queen's most successful season this century and putting Her Majesty among the season's top 20 owners. Among the winners were Group 3 scorers Light Refrain and Reach For The Moon, the latter winning the Solario Stakes and finishing second in the Champagne Stakes, showing smart form and fuelling hopes that he might prove a classic contender in 2022. At a lower level, but making a good contribution to his owner's total nonetheless, was Wink of An Eye, who ran up a four-timer in middle-distance handicaps in the summer for William Haggas and improved into a useful three-year-old.

We'll therefore be hoping that his younger sister Discretion develops along similar lines during her own three-year-old season. Wink of An Eye had three runs at two without looking anything out of the ordinary, but there was plenty of promise in Discretion's sole start last year which came in a novice at Salisbury at the end of September. Soft conditions over the mile made it a day for staying types and the conditions seemed to stretch Discretion's stamina. She shaped well, though, overcoming a bump at the start to chase the leaders and then having to switch over two furlongs out before weakening in the final furlong. Beaten around eight lengths behind the winner Wind Your Neck In, Discretion therefore shaped better than finishing fifth of 13 suggests and she can be expected to improve on that initial effort, possibly by a lot. While Discretion wasn't seen out again, several of the other principals either won or ran well in their subsequent starts.

As well as being a sister to Wink of An Eye, who has won at up to 11 furlongs, Discretion is a half-sister to three more winners, including another useful type, Merlin, a winner at six and seven furlongs. Their dam Momentary, a granddaughter of the Queen's Oaks runner-up Flight of Fancy, was also useful, gaining her only win in a listed race at Newbury over a mile and a quarter on just her second start. This has been a particularly successful family for the Royal Studs as Reach For The Moon is out of a sister to Flight of Fancy. Discretion will stay at least a mile and a quarter and should be well up to winning races for the latest father-and-son training partnership, with Harry Charlton becoming joint licence-holder at Beckhampton this year with father Roger. ***Harry & Roger Charlton***

Conclusion: *Shaped better than the bare result in testing conditions for her sole start at two and it is encouraging that her brother made good progress in handicaps at three last year*

Educator **92p**

3 br.c. Deep Impact (Jpn) – Diploma (Dubawi (Ire))
2021 7g 8m^2 8.2f* Sep 25

One of the great frustrations that follows the publication of a Horses To Follow list is seeing a selection running in races that we at Timeform believe to be unsuitable. We can't choose which races our selections run in, but we can tilt the scales in our favour by siding with trainers who we know will correctly identify their horse's optimum conditions and campaign them in a sensible fashion.

William Haggas is an absolute master of his craft and it is no coincidence that so many of his horses feature in the *Fifty*. Despite being widely regarded as one of the very best there is, you could still turn a level-stake profit over the last five seasons by backing Haggas' three-year-old handicappers in races run over a mile and a quarter or further. Backing such types would have resulted in 77 winners from 277 runners at an exceptional strike-rate of near 28% and a profit of £15.96 to a £1 level stake.

One Haggas-trained three-year-old who we have high hopes for in middle-distance handicaps this season is the progressive Educator. Far too green to do himself justice on debut in a seven-furlong maiden at Newbury in August, he showed the benefit of that experience with a much-improved display on his next outing, shaping like the best prospect in the field when edged out in a one-mile maiden at Goodwood after getting racing a long way out. Educator was fitted with cheekpieces for his next start in a one-mile novice at Haydock and he improved again to get off the mark, showing a good attitude under pressure to fend off a strong challenge from the runner-up, Asean Legend (who has subsequently left Hugo Palmer and joined Haggas, incidentally).

Educator boasts a smart pedigree, being by Deep Impact out of Diploma, a three-time winner for Sir Michael Stoute who produced her best effort when easily landing a listed race over an extended mile and a quarter at York. Diploma's first progeny, Portfolio, developed into a useful middle-distance handicapper last season and it will be a surprise if his full brother Educator fails to do likewise from an opening BHA mark of 87. ***William Haggas***

Conclusion: *Well-bred sort who was progressive as a two-year-old and looks the type to make a mark in middle-distance handicaps for his top yard*

Eldar Eldarov **98P**

3 b.c. Dubawi (Ire) – All At Sea (Sea The Stars (Ire))
2021 8.3g* Oct 13

Last November, Sakhir Racecourse staged the third running of the valuable Bahrain International Trophy which was won by the popular veteran Lord Glitters, trained in

Britain by David O'Meara. No doubt with its eye on Dubai a bit further down the coast of the Persian Gulf, the Kingdom of Bahrain is keen to raise its own international profile as a racing nation. More surprisingly, perhaps, another sport that is popular in Bahrain is Mixed Martial Arts thanks to the enthusiasm of the King's son Khalid bin Hamad Al Khalifa ('KHK'), who has assembled his own stable of fighters known as the KHK MMA Team. Among its members is the Russian-born welterweight Eldar Eldarov, who currently boasts a record of just two defeats in 15 fights as a professional.

Eldar Eldarov now has an equine namesake—owned by KHK Racing Ltd—who looks as though he too might be hard to beat in future the way he came out fighting on his debut at Nottingham in October. Strong in the betting as the 13/8 favourite in a field of eight for the maiden, most of them newcomers, Eldar Eldarov showed his inexperience early on, racing keenly, but he came through to lead over two furlongs out, was in command with over a furlong to run and was well on top at the finish. Eldar Eldarov pulled five lengths clear of the Mark Johnston-trained runner-up Janoobi, with another making his debut, Clear Day for William Haggas, beaten the same distance back in third. Four races were over the mile at Nottingham that day and his was the quickest of them.

Eldar Eldarov has some way to go to recoup the £480,000 he cost at a breeze-up sale last May, but he has made a fine start. As that price tag suggests, he comes from an excellent family of middle-distance performers that includes Alborada, dual winner of the Champion Stakes for Sir Mark Prescott. That mare's sister Albanova won three Group 1 contests in Germany, a feat matched by her granddaughter Alpinista last season. Eldar Eldarov is out of Albanova's daughter All At Sea, a smart filly who won three listed races at around a mile and a quarter in France. Quoted in some lists for the Derby, mostly at 40/1, Eldar Eldarov will stay a mile and a quarter, possibly a mile and a half, and with plenty of improvement to come is very much one to follow in 2022.

Roger Varian

Conclusion: *Expensive breeze-up purchase who was all the rage for his debut and duly won in the manner of a colt destined for better things as a three-year-old*

Filistine (Ire) 89p

3 b.c. Almanzor (Fr) – Desire To Win (Ire) (Lawman (Fr))

2021 7d² 7g* Oct 29

John Gosden trained the leading British hope for the 2016 Champion Stakes, Jack Hobbs, but he was beaten into third behind a couple of top-notchers from overseas, the French colt Almanzor and the Ballydoyle filly Found, who had won the Arc less than a fortnight earlier. Almanzor had already beaten Found in the previous month's Irish Champion Stakes and he won his first Group 1 for Jean-Claude Rouget when successful in the Prix du Jockey Club. Almanzor, now at stud in France, had his first crop of two-year-olds running for him in 2021 and a handful of them won races in Britain, including Filistine for the Gosden stable.

Almanzor won his first three races as a two-year-old but improved markedly at three as the year went on. If Filistine can do the same and build on a promising start at two, then he's an exciting prospect for this year. Even though he was weak in the market near the off, enough was expected of him on his debut in a maiden at Newmarket at the beginning of October for him to be sent off the 7/4 favourite. He didn't win, but he shaped with plenty of encouragement in a field made up mostly of newcomers and finished a length second to another debutant, Al Mubhir, trained by William Haggas. Filistine took a keen hold before coming through to lead over a furlong out and was headed only in the final 50 yards.

That form looked good enough to win most maiden or novice events and Filistine duly needed only to repeat that effort to go one better back at Newmarket in a novice at the end of the month. Filistine landed the odds by a neck from the Godolphin newcomer Silent Speech, travelling well before leading well inside the final furlong as the first two pulled six lengths clear of the third. While Filistine didn't run again, time showed that he'd beaten a useful rival as Silent Speech went on to win his next two starts including a race at the Dubai Carnival. Both of Filistine's races were over seven furlongs and he'll stay at least a mile at three.

Filistine is a lengthy colt, like his father was, but angular too with some filling out to do over the winter. He was a £120,000 breeze-up purchase and is the second winner out of his dam after the French winner up to six and a half furlongs, Anfrati, who was by Almanzor's sire Wootton Bassett. Their dam, Desire To Win, was a nine-furlong winner in France and a half-sister to Don Bosco, a smart French horse up to a mile and a quarter. It probably won't have escaped the attention of his trainers that much further down the page in Filistine's pedigree is the name of Enable! ***John & Thady Gosden***

Conclusion: ***Won the second of his two starts at Newmarket at two and looks the type to progress in handicaps over at least a mile***

Franz 86p

3 b.c. Almanzor (Fr) – Gemstone (Ire) (Galileo (Ire))
2021 8.2d* Oct 15

Gemstone was a useful performer on the racecourse, winning at listed level as a juvenile, but she's made more of a mark in her second career as a broodmare. A daughter of Galileo out of a close relation to Irish 2000 Guineas winner Bachelor Duke, Gemstone has produced seven foals who have hit the track, with the highest-rated of those being UAE Jewel. UAE Jewel quickly established himself as a smart performer in 2019, justifying odds-on favouritism in the Wood Ditton before landing the odds with a ready success in a listed race over a mile and a quarter which earned him a Timeform rating of 118p. Admittedly, he had only one more run at the backend of that campaign and wasn't seen again, but the likeable Nugget soon picked up the baton for Gemstone as he progressed nicely through the handicap ranks, winning on four occasions across the 2020 and 2021 campaigns, earning a Timeform rating of 114.

The latest of Gemstone's runners also has plenty of potential as Franz created a good impression when making a winning start at Haydock in October. That novice event over a mile looked like a decent affair as there were some leading yards represented and some nice pedigrees on show, but Franz knuckled down well inside the final furlong and got the verdict by half a length. Franz is in good hands with Kevin Ryan, who views him as the type to come into his own at three, and he has plenty of untapped potential. His sire Almanzor produced his best form over a mile and a quarter, and Franz should have no problem staying that far. ***Kevin Ryan***

Conclusion: ***Well-bred sort who created a good impression when winning on debut at Haydock, looking the type to develop into a useful performer at around a mile and a quarter at three***

Gaassee (Ire) 108p

4 b.c. Sea The Stars (Ire) – Oojooba (Monsun (Ger))

2021 p10g³ 10.3v* t10.2s* p12s* Dec 15

The return of the top-class miler Baaeed, unbeaten in six career starts to date, will be something to look forward to in 2022, but the fact his trainer William Haggas appears in these pages more than any other trainer tells you that there is much besides to keep him occupied, with Gaassee, in particular, appealing as just the type to climb the ranks. By Sea The Stars, like Baaeed, out of a dam who was herself a daughter of the 1000 Guineas winner Ameerat, Gaassee is certainly bred to be useful and having not seen the racecourse at two—not until the September of his three-year-old season, in fact—he soon set about making up for lost time.

Gaassee made his belated debut in a Lingfield maiden over a mile and a quarter. He was strong in the betting and duly shaped with plenty of promise amidst greenness, getting outpaced three furlongs out and then looking raw on the home turn before finishing nicely to take third behind Emblem Empire. Just over a week later the education continued at Chester and Gaassee was a different proposition this time. He was able to dictate matters but still looked a good prospect as he opened his account in emphatic fashion, powering clear in the straight to win by 15 lengths. It was harder work at Newcastle next time, switched to the tapeta under a penalty in another novice event over a mile and a quarter. Tom Marquand never looked particularly comfortable throughout a stop-start contest but, having been tapped for toe when the tempo did increase three out, his partner found his stride in time to go on inside the distance and beat Hathlool by a length and a half.

Gaassee was given an opening BHA mark of 85 afterwards, but there was no waiting for next year with him. While most were putting up Christmas trees or wrapping presents, he was stepped up in trip to a mile and a half for his handicap debut at Kempton. Gaassee had promised to be suited by further and so it proved as, after being produced to lead two furlongs out, he quickly asserted to land the spoils by five lengths with plenty in hand. The message to the handicapper was catch me if you can and Gaassee did go up 9 lb in the weights for that success, but it would be a major surprise if he wasn't able to progress some way past that. After all, he heads into 2022 unexposed over middle-distances and in the best of hands—there is likely to be some good days to come with another exciting son of Sea The Stars housed at Somerville Lodge. ***William Haggas***

Conclusion: *Lightly raced sort who quickly reached a useful level last season and should have even more to offer as a four-year-old, representing a yard that has excelled with similar types in the past*

Girl On Film (Fr) 89p

3 b.f. Dabirsim (Fr) – Pretty Paper (Ire) (Medaglia d'Oro (USA))
2021 7g* 7m^5 Sep 24

Canadian owners John and Tanya Gunther had a year to remember on both sides of the Atlantic in 2018. As well as having their colours carried to victory at Royal Ascot by Without Parole in the St James's Palace Stakes, they were also the breeders of that year's American Triple Crown winner Justify, who retired unbeaten in six starts and was named US Horse of the Year. With Girl On Film, the father and daughter now look to have a promising filly who could make more of an impact in pattern company than she was able to show when first tried at Group 2 level last year.

Girl On Film made a winning debut at Newmarket in August against nine other newcomers. She was well backed beforehand as the 7/4 favourite and, despite showing inexperience, there was plenty to like about the way she finished the race, taking command inside the final furlong. Overall, there didn't prove to be much strength in depth in the race, certainly not by Newmarket standards, though the third home, Tezzaray, had won a Grade 3 in the USA by the end of the year. While there were lesser options open to Girl On Film, it seemed significant that she was pitched straight into pattern company for the Rockfel Stakes back at Newmarket the following month. As a filly who had raced only once, her profile contrasted sharply with the trio who filled the first three places; between them, Hello You, Cachet and Oscula ran 25 times

Girl On Film (second right, white cap) wasn't seen to best effect in the Rockfel

as two-year-olds, all three of them having contested the Albany Stakes at Royal Ascot back in June as their first pattern race. The first three held those positions throughout, with the much more patiently ridden Girl On Film never on terms in keeping on for fifth and again running green when shaken up.

Girl On Film is by Dabirsim, a dual Group 1 winner in France as a two-year-old, and she is a half-sister to a couple of other winners, including the useful Love And Thunder who won over a mile, a distance Girl On Film will stay herself. Her unraced dam is a half-sister to the smart French colt Bookrunner, who was considered good enough to contest the 2000 Guineas. Girl On Film's Rockfel effort was an improvement on her debut form and, a rangy filly with scope, she looks sure to make a better three-year-old and could well prove the best filly in the Rockfel field in the longer term. ***Ralph Beckett***

Conclusion: ***Lacked experience and the run of the race when tried in the Rockfel Stakes on just her second start and physically looks the type to do better as a three-year-old***

Gnat Alley (Ire) 73

3 gr.f. Caravaggio (USA) – Winter Snow (Ire) (Raven's Pass (USA))

2021 5m^4 5d^4 5g 5m^4 6.5m^4 6m* Sep 22

It took Gnat Alley until her sixth and final start of 2021 to win a race, but she wasn't winning out of turn at Redcar in September and, now that she's off the mark, we think there'll be further wins to come from her in handicaps this year. She first caught the eye on her nursery debut at Ripon at the end of August. That was over five furlongs, the same distance as her three outings the previous month, though she hadn't given the impression that a real test of speed was what she needed. Gnat Alley finished fourth at Beverley on her first two starts, very green for her debut and then well backed on her second start when showing a bit more, but her third outing at Pontefract was a backward step.

Sent off favourite at Ripon, however, Gnat Alley shaped with a lot more encouragement despite being kept to the minimum trip. Soon detached after rearing leaving the stalls, she began to progress from halfway and picked her way through for a staying-on fourth, passing the post just a length and a half or so behind the winner Mereside Angel and likely to have finished closer still with a better start. Nine days later, Gnat Alley was stepped up in trip for the first time for the valuable 'Carrie Red' Fillies Nursery at Doncaster over six and a half furlongs. Running off bottom weight, she didn't run badly to finish fourth again but once more shaped as though she had more ability than she was able to show. Another awkward start didn't help matters and, after racing freely, she could only keep on gradually without proving a threat to useful winner Allayaali.

Things went much more Gnat Alley's way at Redcar and she showed some improvement as a result. She was away on terms this time and, while she was undoubtedly helped by the antics of runner-up Prodigious Blue, who hung right across the track when taking the lead, she finished her race off so strongly to beat him by a length and a half that she might have won no matter what, shaping as though she'll stay at least seven furlongs. The rather leggy Gnat Alley is a half-sister to the fairly useful mile winner Perisher, while their dam is a once-raced half-sister to Glen Shiel, whose biggest win came in the British Champions Sprint Stakes in 2020 but who had winning form at up to nine furlongs in France earlier in his career. ***Tim Easterby***

Conclusion: ***Confirmed earlier promise in nurseries when getting her head in front on her final start last year and should have more to offer in handicaps over seven furlongs plus***

Golden Lyra (Ire) 89p

3 ch.f. Lope de Vega (Ire) – Sea The Sun (Ger) (Sea The Stars (Ire))
2021 7g* Oct 30

William Haggas has trained plenty of good horses in the Sunderland Holding Inc silks in recent seasons, many of those to race in the yellow colours with the purple star being daughters of Sea The Stars. Much the best of those fillies was Sea of Class, winner of the Irish Oaks and Yorkshire Oaks in 2018 before coming from a long way back and failing by just a short neck to collar Enable in the Prix de l'Arc de Triomphe.

Sunderland Holding is the name of the breeding operation of the Tsui family and it was in variations of the same yellow and purple silks that Sea The Stars won the Arc in 2009 for Christopher Tsui, just as that colt's dam Urban Sea had done for his father David in 1993.

The latest promising filly to debut for the operation is Golden Lyra, who isn't by Sea The Stars herself but is out of one of his daughters. Golden Lyra was only third choice in the betting behind a couple of other newcomers from top yards—Nashwa for John and Thady Gosden and Carnival Girl for Charlie Appleby—in a fillies' novice at Newmarket at the end of October, but she showed both that pair a clean pair of heels in running out a ready winner. Always prominent, Golden Lyra took up the running under two furlongs out and was in command in the final furlong. One of the few in the race with some prior experience, Centrallia for Ralph Beckett, was five lengths back in second with Nashwa and Carnival Girl completing the frame.

Golden Lyra made enough of an impression at Newmarket to figure in the Oaks betting at 20/1 or 25/1 with most firms. Her sire Lope de Vega isn't particularly noted for producing horses who excel over a mile and a half, though one of his daughters, Manuela de Vega, did win the Lancashire Oaks. There's no shortage of stamina on the dam's side of Golden Lyra's pedigree and her useful year-older half-brother Going Gone (who is by Le Havre) won a handicap over a mile and a half at Newmarket just a day before Golden Lyra made her debut there. While their dam Sea The Sun was unraced, she is a sister to the German Derby winner Sea The Moon, and their grandam, also unraced, was a sister to two more winners of the same race, Samum and Schiaparelli. A step up to a mile and a quarter in the spring should reveal plenty more about Golden Lyra's potential stamina, and she has the makings of a useful filly at the very least. ***William Haggas***

Conclusion: *Well-bred filly representing connections who have had plenty of success with similar types in recent seasons and has a bright future herself judging from a clear-cut win on her Newmarket debut*

Great Ambassador 114p

5 ch.g. Exceed And Excel (Aus) – Snoqualmie Girl (Ire) (Montjeu (Ire))
2021 p6d* 6m^3 6v^3 6m* 6g* 6g^2 Sep 18

Last season's leading sprinter Starman has been retired to start a stallion career this spring, but his trainer Ed Walker could have one to replace his July Cup winner in the top sprints this year in the shape of Great Ambassador. He gained the last of his three wins in 2021 in the Garrowby Stakes at York in September, a listed contest which Starman himself had won the previous season before developing into a high-class sprinter last

Great Ambassador (No. 21) finishes a close-up third in the Stewards' Cup

year. Although a five-year-old, Great Ambassador remains unexposed as a sprinter as he'd spent much of his early career for Ralph Beckett running over slightly longer trips.

Great Ambassador joined Walker after being bought for 40,000 guineas and connections got some return on their investment at the first opportunity when he made a successful debut for them in a handicap at Kempton in March. He won comfortably, looking well suited by the drop back to six furlongs in a well-run race. The emphasis was a bit too much on speed when he finished third at Newmarket next time and he then missed the Wokingham because of softish ground at Royal Ascot which also ruled Starman out of the Diamond Jubilee.

However, conditions were much softer for his next race, the Stewards' Cup at Goodwood, and they posed no problems for Great Ambassador, who ran right up to his best to finish a length third to Commanche Falls, deserving extra credit as he raced in the smaller far-side group. An impressive win back on firmer ground at Newmarket followed in August before his win over just three rivals in the Garrowby at York. For his final start of the year, Great Ambassador was returned to the much more competitive scenario of one of the season's biggest sprint handicaps and, as in the Stewards' Cup, he acquitted himself very well in defeat in the Ayr Gold Cup for which he started the 3/1 favourite. Travelling fluently, he made steady headway from halfway to lead his group over a furlong out and shot clear of the rest on the far side of the track. However, that was only good enough for second place, with the winner Bielsa racing on his own up the stand side.

Like Starman, Great Ambassador is very much a sprinting type on looks, being a big, strong gelding. With further progress to come, races like the Abernant Stakes at Newmarket and/or the Duke of York, which Starman also won last year, look like suitable early-season targets for him. His run on heavy ground in the Stewards' Cup suggests connections won't have to worry too much about softer conditions for Great Ambassador in future. ***Ed Walker***

Conclusion: *Progressive sprinter who was placed in the Stewards' Cup and Ayr Gold Cup last year and looks all set to leave handicap company behind with further improvement to come in 2022*

Hasty Sailor (Ire) 107

5 b.g. Fastnet Rock (Aus) – Galileano (Ire) (Galileo (Ire))

2021 11.9m³ t12.4s² t12.4s* t12.2s* Oct 16

Sir Michael Stoute is famed for his patient approach, but it is interesting to note that in the last five seasons only three horses aged five or older have represented him in handicap company. If Stoute has kept a horse in training at five it is usually because they are deemed to be of group-race potential, so that bodes well for the prospects of Hasty Sailor, who was withdrawn from October's Tattersalls Horses In Training Sale.

Hasty Sailor had run out an impressive winner of a handicap over a mile and a half at Wolverhampton nine days before the start of the auction, defying a BHA mark of 85 by three and three quarter lengths with plenty in hand. The form of his previous success at Newcastle—when he turned the tables on fellow *Fifty* member Second Slip—had worked out well, but his performance at Wolverhampton represented another big step forward and marked him down as a rapid improver who would remain of firm interest.

Hasty Sailor has a good turn of foot for a middle-distance performer and that is a potent asset on the all-weather, the surface on which he has shown his best form. However, there's little reason to think he won't prove as effective on turf (his first attempt on turf was on his debut in 2020 and his second attempt was on his reappearance last season). On five of Hasty Sailor's seven starts Timeform's reporter has noted him taking a keen hold or travelling strongly. That suggests he is not in need of a step up in trip, but it's worth noting his dam is stoutly bred and won over a mile and three quarters, so there is potential that he will stay further. ***Sir Michael Stoute***

Conclusion: *Lightly-raced five-year-old who finished last season on a sharp upward curve, so one to be interested in for a valuable middle-distance handicap and possibly even minor group races*

Hebrides (Ire) 88p

Mehmas (Ire) – Woodland Maiden (Ire) (Mastercraftsman (Ire))

2021 6.5v^3 6s* Nov 6

William Haggas has done well with the horses he has trained for the Highclere Thoroughbred Racing syndicates over the years. Among them are Approve, winner of the Norfolk Stakes and Gimcrack, Conquest, another Gimcrack winner who went on to win the Stewards' Cup, and Raucous, who was placed in the same two races. It's still early days for the same connections' Hebrides, but if the promise he showed at two is anything to go by, he too could make up into an above-average sprinter.

Hebrides was bought for 105,000 guineas from the Craven Breeze Up Sale in the spring, but he was given plenty of time and didn't appear until the final weeks of the turf season. He produced a promising first effort in difficult conditions for a newcomer as the going was heavy at Newbury. Held up after a slow start, Hebrides made a big move to get into contention, going second with a furlong to run, but he couldn't sustain his effort and wound up finishing just over two lengths behind the winner American Kestrel in third. Hebrides had been sent off favourite at Newbury and he was odds on to get off the mark at the second attempt in another maiden on November Handicap day at Doncaster just over a fortnight later. He did so in taking fashion. Travelling smoothly in touch, he led on the bridle over a furlong out and just needed to be pushed out by Tom Marquand to gain an easy win by a length and three quarters from the newcomer Taratari. Although both his starts have been in the mud, Hebrides gives the impression he'll be as effective on a sounder surface.

Hebrides, who was gelded after Doncaster, comes from the second crop of the July and Richmond Stakes winner Mehmas, who broke records as the leading first-season sire in 2020 when his offspring included the Richmond and Middle Park winner Supremacy and the Gimcrack winner Minzaal. He had the Gimcrack winner again in his latest crop of two-year-olds when Lusail was successful at York. Although neither his dam nor grandam ran, there's also speed in the bottom half of Hebrides' pedigree as his grandam was a half-sister to the Coventry Stakes winner CD Europe, while his dam is a half-sister to Iveagh Gardens, who must be one of the quickest horses to carry the J. P. McManus colours as she won the Group 3 Athasi Stakes over seven furlongs at the Curragh. This is also the family of the smart performer at up to a mile and a quarter Tenor, who was successful for Highclere early in his career. ***William Haggas***

Conclusion: *Confirmed debut promise when an easy winner on his final start at two and looks a useful sprinter in the making*

Injazati (Ire) 106

4 ch.c. Night of Thunder (Ire) – Mathanora (Ire) (Anabaa (USA))
2021 8d^3 9s^3 10.2m* t10.2s* 10g* 12d^5 Oct 8

Few decisions regarding the racing programme are met with universal approval, but everyone will surely agree that the addition of the Old Rowley Cup to the autumn calendar has been an unqualified success. The valuable handicap run over a mile and a half for three-year-olds is always a fantastic punting puzzle which usually provides a rock-solid piece of form, and the early signs are that the latest edition was an especially strong contest. The winner Siskany may have been beaten on his next couple of outings, but he showed himself to be a very smart performer when bolting up in a listed race at Meydan in January. The runner-up at Newmarket, Farhan, justified favouritism in the competitive November Handicap on his next start, while third-placed Candleford has also won impressively since the Old Rowley Cup.

In truth, there are a host of potential Horses To Follow you could select from the Old Rowley Cup, but the one we're siding with is fifth-placed Injazati, who ultimately failed to meet expectations at Newmarket having been sent off the 7/2 second favourite, shaping like he failed to stay on his first crack at a mile and a half. However, there were mitigating factors as he raced prominently in a race run at an end-to-end gallop, while

Injazati is clear of his rivals at Newbury

he also made his move earlier than ideal, hitting the front still going strongly three furlongs from home. Injazati arrived at Newmarket firmly on the up having completed a hat-trick at a mile and a quarter, following up a novice win at Nottingham with handicap victories at Newcastle and Newbury, showing improved form on each occasion.

The victory at Newbury was achieved in the Dubai Duty Free Handicap, a race which has a rich history, and the style of that two-length success identified Injazati as being a horse still some way ahead of his mark. Whilst unable to prove that point under unfavourable circumstances in a red-hot race at Newmarket, he is well worth another crack at a mile and a half and remains with potential. ***Charlie Fellowes***

Conclusion: *Showed rapid progress at three, completing a hat-trick over a mile and a quarter before finishing a promising fifth in a strong race at Newmarket on his first attempt at a mile and a half*

Koy Koy

93p

3 b.c. Acclamation – Lynique (Ire) (Dylan Thomas (Ire))

2021 $6g^5$ $7m^2$ 7g* Sep 18

Koy Koy's three runs at two have laid the foundations for what is expected to be a successful campaign this year. Handicaps look the way to go with him, at least to begin with, though the fact that he has been given an entry in the Irish 2000 Guineas indicates that connections believe he has potential at a higher level. The race he won on his final start wasn't the strongest for an autumn two-year-old contest at Newbury and he had much the best form already in the 12-runner novice, but there was no arguing with the way Koy Koy went about winning it. Under a no-nonsense ride from Oisin Murphy, Koy Koy made all the running and, once shaken up from two furlongs out, drew clear to land the odds by six and a half lengths with a couple of outsiders taking the places.

Koy Koy had made his debut over six furlongs at Salisbury before stepping up to seven for his other two starts. He produced a promising first effort and, though green under pressure, seemed to be getting the hang of things late on as he finished fifth behind a striking winner in Ribhi, who went on to show useful form. Koy Koy duly improved a good deal for that initial experience on his next start at Ascot. That proved a very one-sided contest, with the Gosdens' odds-on favourite Saga making all the running, though Koy Koy fared best of the rest to be beaten a length and a half into second, staying on without troubling the winner. The time of the race was good, and Saga's earlier form reads extremely well given that he'd found only two of Godolphin's very best two-year-olds, Modern Games and Coroebus, too good for him in his previous starts.

Being a tall, unfurnished colt, Koy Koy has the physical scope to develop at three. He cost 58,000 guineas as a yearling and his pedigree combines speed from his sire Acclamation with more stamina on his dam's side. His dam, Lynique, finished down the field on her only start, but she had some good relatives, including her sister Tannery, a Group 3 winner in Ireland who went on to win the Grade 1 E. P. Taylor Stakes in Canada over a mile and a quarter. Lynique was from a Ballymacoll Stud family as she was out of a half-sister to the very smart middle-distance stayer Gamut, whose wins for Sir Michael Stoute included the Grand Prix de Saint-Cloud. Koy Koy himself should have no trouble staying a mile. ***Andrew Balding***

Conclusion: ***Showed promise before running out a clear-cut winner on his final start and looks capable of making into a useful handicapper at around a mile***

Light Infantry (Fr) 109p

3 ch.c. Fast Company (Ire) – Lights On Me (Kyllachy)
2021 6m* 7v* Oct 23

Run at Newbury's final Flat meeting of the year towards the end of October, the Horris Hill Stakes is one of the last opportunities in Britain for a two-year-old to pick up a pattern race. It's been a long time since it was last won by a future classic winner—that was Tirol in 1989 who went on to win the 2000 Guineas the following spring for Richard Hannon senior—but more recently the Horris Hill was won by Mohaather, who later proved himself a high-class miler for Marcus Tregoning when an impressive winner of the Sussex Stakes in 2020. As is often the case given the time of year, the latest Horris Hill was run in testing conditions which proved too much for the Godolphin favourite Noble Truth but proved no problem at all for David Simcock's colt Light Infantry.

Offspring of Light Infantry's sire, the Dewhurst Stakes runner-up Fast Company, often relish soft or heavy ground and Light Infantry put up a much-improved effort at Newbury. As it was just his second outing, Light Infantry was entitled to show the odd sign of greenness after a slow start, but he saw out the testing seven furlongs really well, making good headway over a furlong out before staying on to lead in the final 100 yards. He was driven out to beat another unexposed colt, Cresta, by a length and a half, with the favourite weakening into fourth once Light Infantry had headed him. Conditions were much firmer for his debut when, despite pulling hard early on, Light Infantry shot clear to win a novice over six furlongs at Yarmouth in September by six and a half lengths, looking the useful prospect he proved to be at Newbury.

Light Infantry was a £82,000 purchase at the breeze-up sales and comes from a family which has mostly distinguished itself abroad. His dam Lights On Me won four races at up to around a mile in Italy, Germany and Austria, and she has produced one other winner to date, Love Henry, successful over nine furlongs in France. Lights On

Me's siblings include the useful Choose Your Moment, who won a listed race over a mile at Pontefract. Light Infantry looks sure to stay a mile himself and with further improvement to come has the makings of a smart colt. He's available at 33/1 in places for the 2000 Guineas which could look big if he performs well in a trial, though as a French-bred colt who's proven in the mud, perhaps connections will be looking at opportunities for him across the Channel, too. ***David Simcock***

Conclusion: *Bolted up on his debut and looked a potentially smart miler when following up on heavy ground in the Horris Hill Stakes*

Lionel **82P**

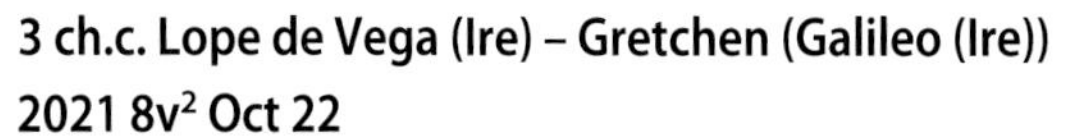

3 ch.c. Lope de Vega (Ire) – Gretchen (Galileo (Ire))

2021 8v^2 Oct 22

Given his dam's high-class middle-distance pedigree and trainer David Menuisier's reputation for taking the steady approach, it bodes extremely well for Lionel's prospects that he showed so much ability when filling the runner-up spot on his debut in a one-mile novice at Newbury towards the backend of last season.

Lionel carries the distinctive pink and white silks of Normandie Stud and he hails from one of the operation's most successful families. His dam, Gretchen, is a granddaughter of Agnus—the first mare purchased by Phillipa Cooper after buying Normandie Stud—and a daughter of the acclaimed Dolores. From eight runners, Dolores produced seven winners, four black-type performers and a Group 1 winner in the shape of Duncan, her highest-rated progeny who dead-heated in the 2011 Irish St Leger.

Gretchen, a daughter of Galileo, was a high achiever herself during a short career, with her five starts including three wins, most notably the Group 2 Park Hill Stakes, over a mile and three quarters, at Doncaster in 2015. Lionel is Gretchen's first foal to hit the track and he shaped with clear promise at Newbury, making a big, eye-catching move out wide to dispute the lead inside the final furlong before ultimately coming off second best against a rival who had the benefit of previous experience.

Menuisier surprisingly posts a level-stake profit with his two-year-old debutants in the past five seasons, but a 6% strike rate with such types is probably the better guide as to how ready he tends to get his juveniles at the first attempt. With that in mind, Lionel, who has the Timeform large 'P' attached to his rating, looks the type to make significant improvement given time, and he'll be suited by stepping up to at least a mile and a quarter. ***David Menuisier***

Conclusion: *Made a highly encouraging debut on his only start at two and his high-class pedigree allied with the trainer's patient approach suggests significant improvement is likely*

Simon Baker (Lionel): *"Lionel showed sufficient promise on his debut at Newbury last backend to think he was the best horse in that race—he was comfortably the fastest of the bunch through the final three furlongs—and that, allied with his smart middle-distance breeding, gives him the look of a most exciting long-term prospect for a trainer in David Menuisier who excels at the patient approach."*

Magisterial (Ire) 93p

3 b.c. Frankel – Hoity Toity (Darshaan)

2021 8m^{4} 8.2d* Oct 15

Who better than a horse named Stradivarius to prove there's truth in the saying 'there's many a good tune played on an old fiddle'? Stradivarius will be attempting to do just that at the age of eight this year, and while a fourth Gold Cup eluded him in 2021, a third Lonsdale Cup at York and a second Doncaster Cup last season was still a good return for Bjorn Nielsen's entire. His owner will have plenty of big days to look back on when the time does come for Stradivarius to be retired, but, as far as the future is concerned, Nielsen and the Gosdens should also have plenty to look forward to with Magisterial whose career is only just getting under way.

It took Stradivarius until his third start as a two-year-old to get his head in front, but Magisterial went one better when successful on his second outing in a novice at

Magisterial represents the same connections as star stayer Stradivarius

Haydock in October. He stood out on the form of his debut effort when an eye-catching fourth behind Subastar in a Newmarket maiden the previous month and duly won decisively at Haydock. Sent off odds on, Magisterial was still green when Oisin Murphy asked him to go about his business but, after travelling fluently in mid-division, he was produced to lead over a furlong out and was driven out to beat second favourite Splendent by a length and a half with something to spare. The runner-up was a winner himself on his next start.

John Gosden trained Frankel's first two classic winners, Anapurna and Logician, winners of the Oaks and St Leger respectively in 2019. Anapurna was beaten a long way at Wolverhampton on her only start at two, while Logician didn't race at all as a two-year-old, so it's not fanciful to think Magisterial, by the same sire who was champion for the first time in 2021, could make into a Derby contender as he's certainly bred to get the trip. His full sister Flaunt won over just short of a mile and a half at Windsor last year, but the pick of Magisterial's siblings is the very smart Ballydoyle filly Lillie Langtry, who won the Coronation Stakes and Matron Stakes. She has since proved a top broodmare as well, producing an even better filly than she was herself in Minding, whose Group 1 wins included the 1000 Guineas and Oaks in 2016, as well as last year's Irish 1000 Guineas winner Empress Josephine. There are classic hopes too for Lillie Langtry's current three-year-old filly Tuesday so, who knows, the family could be represented in both classics at Epsom in June. ***John & Thady Gosden***

Conclusion: *Bred in the purple and confirmed debut promise when a ready winner at Haydock on his second start, so entitled to begin 2022 with hopes that he'll develop into a Derby contender*

Manila Scouse 85

3 b.g. Aclaim (Ire) – Forever Excel (Ire) (Excelebration (Ire))

2021 5d^5 5.1v^2 6v^2 5d* Oct 26

Tim Easterby has set new personal bests for number of winners in three of the last four years—the understandable exception was the Covid-hit season of 2020—and his total of 137 in 2021 came with earnings which put him in the top 10 in the trainers' championship. One who should be paying his way for the stable—and our *Fifty*—this year is Manila Scouse, who is one to look out for in sprint handicaps.

Although showing plenty of speed, Manila Scouse was by no means an early two-year-old and he didn't make his debut until mid-September when shaping better than the bare result after meeting trouble to take fifth in a maiden at Beverley. He duly improved on that but had to settle for second in novice events on his next couple of starts at Chester and Pontefract. At Chester he failed by just a head to reel in the filly Designer, shaping as though a step up to six furlongs would suit, but when even-money favourite over that trip at Pontefract, he went down by a length and three quarters to another filly, Greenbarn, after making much of the running. Those were fairly useful efforts in defeat, though, and it wasn't long before Manila Scouse was found a good opportunity to get his head in front, back at five furlongs, in a novice at Catterick just eight days after Pontefract. Manila Scouse and the only previous winner in the field, Lotus Rose, were the only two who really ever looked like winning, the pair of them forcing the pace on the stand side, and it was Manila Scouse who proved the stronger in the closing stages to win by a length and three quarters. Manila Scouse wore a tongue tie for the first time at Catterick and has been gelded since that appearance.

Manila Scouse looks well bought as he cost just £9,000 as a yearling and comes from the first crop of the very smart Aclaim, who won at up to a mile but was best at around seven furlongs. His dam showed little in just a couple of starts but one of her half-brothers, Doctor Sardonicus, was a smart sprinter on the all-weather, while her own dam, Never A Doubt, was a speedy two-year-old, winning the Prix Robert Papin and finishing second in the Queen Mary at Royal Ascot. ***Tim Easterby***

Conclusion: *Posted good efforts in defeat before getting off the mark on his final start at two and looks the type to hold his own in sprint handicaps in the North this year*

Morning Poem 85p

3 b.f. Kingman – Mill Springs (Shirocco (Ger))
2021 p8s* Nov 10

'The second half of my career has been a lot better than the first! I've got John Gosden to thank for that, he's been an unbelievable friend and supporter for a long time and it's down to him.' Robert or 'Rab' Havlin was speaking after riding the thousandth winner of his career—appropriately enough for Gosden—at Lingfield in March 2020. Havlin plays a vital role riding work and educating young horses at Clarehaven and, while Frankie Dettori might have enjoyed all the glory on the big days on such stable stars as Cracksman and Enable, it was Havlin who guided both of those horses to their debut successes as two-year-olds. Although he never got to ride him on a racecourse, Kingman was another top-class horse Havlin rode in all his work at home.

Only time will tell whether Kingman's daughter Morning Poem becomes another two-year-old to benefit from Havlin's handling on her racecourse debut before going on to much bigger things, but she certainly looked a useful filly in the making, at least, when successful first time up in a novice at Kempton in November. At 10/1, Morning Poem was actually the longer priced of the stable's two runners—the other, Lady Hamilton, having had the benefit of a run already—but she overcame her inexperience to win in taking fashion in the end. After a slow start, she had a lot of ground to make up in the straight but got the hang of things in the closing stages and stayed on to lead close home for a half-length win over favourite Lady Clementine, who almost managed to make all.

Kingman was never tried beyond a mile, whereas, if Morning Poem takes after her dam, no distance will be too far for her. Also trained by Gosden, Mill Springs was a thorough stayer as she proved when producing a career best to finish third under Dettori in the Ascot Stakes over two and a half miles on soft ground. However, both her career victories came with Havlin in the saddle, including a listed race at the same track over a mile and three quarters. Mill Springs' half-sister Monturani was also placed at Royal Ascot, albeit over a mile in the Windsor Forest Stakes (she was by sprinter Indian Ridge), while their dam Mezzogiorno, who also carried Mrs Philipps' colours, finished third in the Oaks. It remains to be seen how far Morning Poem stays herself, but she should have no trouble getting a mile and a quarter at the very least. She's sure to progress and win more races. ***John & Thady Gosden***

Conclusion: ***Overcame greenness to win cosily in the end on her sole start at two and sure to progress for her top stable at three, her pedigree an interesting mix of speed and stamina***

Mujtaba 110p

4 b.g. Dubawi (Ire) – Majmu (Aus) (Redoute's Choice (Aus))
2021 8.1g* 7.6g* 8d* Oct 25

Given their reduction in numbers and vast sales at all age groups in the autumn, it's potentially telling which horses Shadwell opted to retain as part of their 'boutique' team for 2022. Mujtaba finds himself in the minority who will continue to sport the famous royal blue silks with white epaulets, and it will be a surprise if he isn't doing so in some good races as a four-year-old. After all, he has already achieved a smart level of form after going unbeaten in three outings last season and the potential is there for him to do better still as he gains more experience.

By Dubawi out of a smart winner in South Africa, Mujtaba was unraced at two and didn't make his first appearance on a racecourse until August when lining up in a novice event over a mile at Chepstow. A weak affair, his sole serious rival was Rani of Jhansi, who had made the frame in all four of her previous starts. She did so again but never threatened to be a match for Mujtaba, who learned on the job and, after being pushed to the front over a furlong out, quickly drew four and a quarter lengths clear of his rival. Turned out again a month later in a Chester novice, Mujtaba didn't need to improve to make it two from two but, in a tactical affair which developed into a two-furlong sprint, there was still plenty to like about the way he reeled in the front-running Ciotog in ready fashion. It was another month before we saw Mujtaba again as he headed to Redcar for his handicap debut, where he was faced with an opening BHA mark of 90 and going softer than good for the first time in his career. There was more substance to this race and again style in the performance, too. Dane O'Neill was in the saddle and his partner came clear from the two-furlong pole to beat another in-form three-year-old in Empirestateofmind by two and a quarter lengths.

It's highly unlikely that we've seen the best of Mujtaba as yet and just the manner of that success at Redcar suggests he is still well handicapped from a BHA mark of 98. He is currently among the ante-post favourites for the Lincoln at Doncaster, a race trainer William Haggas has won three times since 2007, most recently in 2018 with the subsequent Group 1 winner Addeybb. It might be asking too much to hope that Mujtaba can scale similar heights, but he certainly looks the sort to pick up a good handicap or two before his sights are raised. ***William Haggas***

Conclusion: *Three from three in his first season of racing and has the potential to progress beyond handicaps in time*

Pat Jupp (Mujtaba): *"William Haggas took the softly-softly approach with Mujtaba as a three-year-old, only starting him off in late-Summer and avoiding the top tracks, but he still made a big impression in winning all three starts, notably when easily beating another progressive type on his handicap debut at Redcar. He starts the season on a BHA mark of 98 and looks an ideal type to notch a fifth win in the Lincoln for his trainer, with pattern races likely to be on the agenda later in the campaign."*

Nations Pride (Ire) 92p

3 b.c. Teofilo (Ire) – Important Time (Ire) (Oasis Dream)

2021 7g[2] p8g* p10s* Nov 6

Sheikh Mohammed has not seen much of a return on the 3.4 million guineas he spent on Satwa Queen at the 2007 Tattersalls December Mares Sale. At the time that was a European record for a filly or mare in training, but maybe Satwa Queen's grandson Nations Pride will be capable of lifting a big prize in the Godolphin colours in 2022. He's certainly made a very promising start to his career, particularly for a colt who looks as though he's going to be suited by at least a mile and a half.

Nations Pride shaped very well on his debut when running on late for second in a seven-furlong maiden at Yarmouth and, despite a false pace, ran out an impressive winner, by nearly five lengths, of a novice at Lingfield on his next start in October when stepped up to a mile. The pace was modest again when Nations Pride was stepped up to a mile and a quarter for his final start in a conditions race at Chelmsford in November. Facing two rivals trained by Mark Johnston and one for John and Thady

Gosden, Nations Pride landed the odds again in good style, leading two furlongs out and keeping on well for a ready three-length success over one of the Johnston colts Levitate. While Nations Pride's bare form to date is no better than fairly useful, he has given the strong impression that he'll prove quite a bit better than that given the right sort of opportunities at three.

Nations Pride's grandam Satwa Queen showed very smart form in France, ending her racing career there with a win in the Prix de l'Opera after landing another Group 1, the Prix Jean Romanet, for the second year running. The best of her own offspring was Nations Pride's dam Important Time, whose wins included a nine-furlong listed race in Germany. She has produced one other winner so far, Making History, who won a seven-furlong nursery at Leicester for Saeed bin Suroor. Satwa Queen is also the grandam of Lucky Vega, winner of the Phoenix Stakes as a two-year-old before running a close third in last year's 2000 Guineas and then finishing behind Poetic Flare again when runner-up in the St James's Palace Stakes. The stamina that Nations Pride has shown comes from his sire Teofilo, who was responsible for last year's Gold Cup winner Subjectivist and for Godolphin's 2018 Melbourne Cup winner Cross Counter. Teofilo has since won another Melbourne Cup with Twilight Payment, that one out of an Oasis Dream mare like Nations Pride. ***Charlie Appleby***

Conclusion: *Already a mile and a quarter winner at two and looks a very promising middle-distance/staying prospect*

Opera Gift 109p

5 b.g. Nathaniel (Ire) – Opera Glass (Barathea (Ire))
2021 14.2g* May 2

Andrew Balding finished runner-up in the trainers' championship in 2021 when the very smart filly Alcohol Free was the stable's major earner thanks to her Group 1 wins in the Coronation Stakes and Sussex Stakes. Earlier in the year, on the same day that Alcohol Free finished fifth in the 1000 Guineas, her owner Jeff Smith had a runner at Salisbury who looked as though he too was all set to go on to better things later in the season.

Unfortunately, Opera Gift wasn't seen out again after his highly promising return to action in the City Bowl Handicap over a mile and three quarters. Sent off favourite, Opera Gift travelled well close to the pace before David Probert produced him to lead over a furlong out. He was well on top at the line, having two and a quarter lengths to spare over Midnight Legacy with Gumball, a former winner of the race, just a nose back in third. It was all pretty academic as far as Opera Gift was concerned but, for what it's worth, the form worked out really well as both placed horses, along with a couple of others in the seven-strong field, all won their next starts. Opera Gift's next appearance could have been in the Northumberland Plate—he was second favourite and 8/1 ante-post with most firms—but he missed that race and, as we said, the remainder of the season.

That means that Opera Gift has still had only five starts all told as he was a late developer and didn't reach the track until the autumn of his three-year-old season. After getting off the mark on his second start when stepped up to a mile and a half for a maiden at Pontefract, he then followed up at Yarmouth on his handicap debut over the same trip but with the emphasis very much on stamina thanks to the heavy ground. Stepping up to the St Leger trip at Doncaster, he improved again under a penalty for that win when going down by half a length to another progressive type, Ocean Wind, on his final start at three.

Opera Gift is sure to stay two miles when he gets the chance at that trip. One of his half-brothers, Opera Buff, was a fairly useful staying handicapper, but the family's best stayer was his dam's half-brother Grey Shot, who enjoyed a long, varied and successful career at Kingsclere, winning on the Flat, over hurdles and over fences. As well as winning the Goodwood Cup in Jeff Smith's colours, he also won a Kingwell Hurdle and contested a Gold Cup, a Melbourne Cup and a Champion Hurdle. ***Andrew Balding***

Conclusion: *Restricted to just the one start last year, which he won, but remains with plenty of potential for the top staying handicaps*

Outbreak — 91p

3 b.c. Dark Angel (Ire) – Purr Along (Mount Nelson)
2021 p8s² 8g* 8m² Sep 16

The winning machine that is Kingsley Park rolls relentlessly on and, for the tenth time in his career, Mark Johnston recorded a double-century of winners in 2021, something he first achieved in 2009. When Golden Sands won a handicap at Wolverhampton just three days into January, he was the first of what will no doubt be another mammoth total for the Middleham stable this year. But there was some added significance to that win as it was the first for the new official partnership of Charlie and Mark Johnston as joint licencees, though in practice Johnston's son has been heavily involved in the running of the yard for several years.

As well as making his contribution to last year's double-century, Outbreak should be adding to the Johnstons' total this season. Without looking the finished article at two, Outbreak showed fairly useful form in his three starts, all of them novice contests over a mile. He made his debut on the polytrack at Chelmsford in August and showed plenty of ability in pushing the more experienced Claim The Crown close, going down by half a length to Roger Varian's colt who was placed in a Group 3 in France on his next start. 12 days later, Outbreak had no trouble going one better at Salisbury as the even-money favourite, making it a very one-sided contest as he made all the running to win readily by five lengths from Point Lynas despite hanging right in the last couple of furlongs. His final start at Ayr was expected to be another straightforward task—he was sent off at 7/2-on against nine rivals under his penalty as the only winner in the line-up—but having set out to make all again, he was headed in the final 100 yards by Richard Fahey's runner Gorak, who won cosily by a length and three quarters. Conceding 6 lb to that progressive rival was almost certainly a stiffer task than it looked at the time and the defeat doesn't detract from Outbreak's prospects at three.

A 67,000-guinea yearling purchase by Qatar Racing, Outbreak is a half-brother to the useful Starcat, who contested the 2000 Guineas for Hughie Morrison, and to Zuba, a fairly useful handicapper at up to a mile and three quarters. Zuba was by Dubawi, more of a stamina influence than Outbreak's sire Dark Angel. Their dam Purr Along also raced in the Qatar Racing colours after her purchase for a million guineas out of William Muir's stable at the end of her three-year-old season. She made a winning start for new trainer Johnny Murtagh in the Group 3 Lanwades Stud Stakes over a mile at the Curragh. ***Charlie & Mark Johnston***

Conclusion: *Turned over at short odds on his final start but made a good impression overall at two and sure to be found some winning opportunities in handicaps this year*

Paradias (Ger) 80p

3 b.c. Kodiac – Paraisa (Red Ransom (USA))

2021 7g^2 8g^4 8.2d^3 Oct 15

Alan King has broken the £1-million barrier several times over jumps during his career, but 2021 was the first time he has achieved that feat in a season on the Flat. His high-class stayer Trueshan was the stable's main earner from winning the Goodwood Cup and Long Distance Cup, also winning the Prix du Cadran in France in between, while two-year-old Asymmetric chipped in with a valuable win of his own at Goodwood in the Richmond Stakes which says plenty for his trainer's versatility at handling all types of horses, both on the Flat and over jumps.

Paradias wasn't such a precocious two-year-old as Asymmetric, but he showed enough last year to suggest that he's one to follow in 2022. Clearly not too much was expected of Paradias first time up as he was sent off at 20/1 for a newcomers' race at Sandown in August, but he stuck to his task in finishing second of the 11 runners behind the Godolphin colt King of Conquest. That earned Paradias a crack at the following month's Haynes, Hanson & Clark Conditions Stakes at Newbury, a race with a rich history of throwing up good horses. King won it himself with Tritonic two years earlier, that horse now a smart hurdler for the yard, though for Paradias it was a case of flying a bit too high at that stage of his career as he pulled hard in a steadily-run race and finished fourth of the six runners behind Zechariah with King of Conquest, sent off the 5/4 favourite, a place ahead of him again. Kept to a mile, Paradias shaped well with his sights lowered to a novice event at Haydock for his final start and finished two lengths third to newcomer Franz, taking the eye with how far he travelled on the bridle, looming up to lead two furlongs out before being headed in the last half-furlong. He again tended to race freely early on but can be expected to improve further once he learns to relax in his races.

The well-made Paradias, a £100,000 breeze-up purchase, comes from a successful German family. He's a half-brother to a couple of two-year-old winners in Germany and his useful dam Paraisa was a listed winner over a mile there at the same age. Her half-brothers Praiano and Desert Emperor both had good seasons in middle-distance handicaps in Britain last year, while another half-brother, Potemkin, has been a prolific winner in Europe, landing a Group 1 prize in Italy in the Premio Roma. Being by sprinter Kodiac, Paradias will have to settle if he's to prove effective beyond a mile himself. ***Alan King***

Conclusion: *Showed ability in all his two-year-old starts, shaping nicely on his final one when travelling well for a long way*

Ravenscraig Castle 96p

4 gr.g. Nathaniel (Ire) – In The Soup (USA) (Alphabet Soup (USA))
2021 11.2g* 13.1g* 13.9m^3 16d^2 13.9s^4 Oct 8

The owners going by the name of Castle Racing Scotland had three horses run for them on the Flat in Britain last season, all of them trained by Iain Jardine and named after significant landmarks north of the border. One of them was Ravenscraig Castle, who shares his name with a structure in Kirkcaldy dating back to the second half of the fifteenth century, when King James II ordered it to be built as a place of residence for his wife, Queen Mary of Gueldres. Today the castle lies in ruins, but it will be a surprise if the racing career of the equine Ravenscraig Castle meets the same fate in 2022, such was the staying power he showed in five appearances last season.

Ravenscraig Castle achieved just a fair level of form in three starts at two, but he took a big step forward after nine months off and a gelding operation to open his account at Carlisle in July. Making his handicap debut from an opening BHA mark of 69, he was well suited both by the step up in trip and the way things developed, coming from a long way back in a strongly-run race to win by a length and a quarter. Ravenscraig Castle then defied a 4 lb rise in the weights to follow up at Ayr later that month, stepping up to 13 furlongs this time and clearly relishing the extra distance as he overcame unfavourable circumstances to land the spoils by two lengths. The runner-up Fandabidozi had dictated matters to suit him, so it was to Ravenscraig Castle's credit that he was ultimately well on top at the finish after coming under pressure a fair way out.

Despite having easier options in the North open to him in his hat-trick bid, Ravenscraig Castle made his next appearance in the hugely competitive Sky Bet Melrose at York's Ebor Festival, where he ran a stormer on his first try over a mile and three quarters to finish third, doing his best work late on to pass the post just half a length behind the winner Valley Forge. His strength at the finish suggested he would be suited by going up further in trip and he duly showed improved form when filling the runner-up spot over two miles at Musselburgh in September, sticking to his task well to be beaten just three quarters of a length.

Two-mile handicaps are probably where Ravenscraig Castle's future lies in 2022, particularly as he appeared to lack the pace to make more of an impact when fourth on his final start back at York in October, that race coming over the same course and distance as the Melrose. He will start his four-year-old campaign on a BHA mark of 87 and there should be more races to be won with him when the emphasis is firmly on stamina, with the Northumberland Plate appealing as an obvious target. ***Iain Jardine***

Conclusion: *Made significant progress in five starts last season and should have more to offer as a four-year-old when stamina is at a premium*

Simon Walker (Ravenscraig Castle): *"For a horse whose Timeform rating went from 72 to 96 in just five starts as a three-year-old, wins in middling handicaps at Ayr and Carlisle could be deemed a disappointing return for Ravenscraig Castle. It was his subsequent in-frame efforts in much better-quality affairs, however, that marked him down as a stayer to have on side in 2022. He's still to have his stamina properly tested at two miles, undone by a steady gallop and another well-treated one on his only attempt at the trip so far, and it'll be surprising if his Timeform rating isn't closer to 110 by the time the next Flat season concludes."*

Roach Power (Ire) 79p

3 gr.c. Ribchester (Ire) – Evening Time (Ire) (Keltos (Fr))

2021 5.8m^2 7.2d^4 6g^2 Sep 24

Only Godolphin and Shadwell had more winners than King Power Racing in Britain in 2021 and, as the owner's chosen trainer in the North, Tim Easterby has benefitted more than most from the Thai company's massive investment in British racing in recent years. Easterby had a couple of King Power's best horses in 2021, Winter Power and Art Power, both of them very smart sprinters. The three-year-old filly Winter Power won the Nunthorpe at York, while four-year-old colt Art Power made the frame in three Group 1 sprints over six furlongs during the year, as well as winning the Group 3 Renaissance Stakes at the Curragh by five lengths.

If Roach Power shares just some of the ability of his elder half-brother Art Power, therefore, he should be in for a successful three-year-old campaign. The signs were good at two, notably when he ended the year with a narrow defeat at York. Roach Power showed he has plenty of speed himself, travelling well and leading at halfway in the six-furlong novice, but he found the 25/1 shot Another Investment just a neck too good at the line. Roach Power also finished second on his debut in a similar event over Carlisle's stiffer track in August, but he shaped well from off the pace after a slow start and bumped into an above-average rival as the winner, Breeze Easy, went on to be placed in listed races in the autumn. Between Carlisle and York, Roach Power was stepped up to seven furlongs for another novice at Musselburgh, but he didn't improve for the longer trip and still looked green in finishing fourth of the six runners behind Animato.

Roach Power comes from the first crop of high-class miler Ribchester, whose best two-year-olds, Flaming Rib and Gisburn, both did well over six furlongs last year. Roach Power is a half-brother to no fewer than eight winners, Art Power much the best of them but not the only good sprinter among his siblings as useful half-sister Penny Pepper won the Group 3 Ballyogan Stakes at the Curragh. Their dam Evening Time was a smart sprinter in Ireland, her three wins all gained by wide margins on soft ground over six furlongs, including listed races at both two and three, and she had a half-brother in Italy, Distinctly Dancer, who was a smart sprinter himself. ***Tim Easterby***

Conclusion: ***Half-brother to Art Power, a very smart sprinter for the same connections, and showed enough at two to suggest he'll be up to winning races over similar trips this season***

Rogue Bear (Ire) 96p

4 br.g. Kodiac – Rancho Montoya (Ire) (High Chaparral (Ire))

2021 6m* 6s³ 7m⁴ 8.3s* 8.3g* Oct 27

The Rogues Gallery Racing Club can count a few familiar faces among its members. They include Rishi Persad, one of the most recognisable sports broadcasters on television, as well as Vinnie Jones, who reinvented himself as an actor after retiring from professional football and a career spanning successful spells with the likes of Leeds United and Wimbledon. Jones also played 35 games in the red and white stripes of Sheffield United, scoring two goals in the First Division in the 1990/91 season.

Rogue Bear went one better than Jones by getting on the scoresheet three times in the red and white silks of The Rogues Gallery in 2021. Rogue Bear is quite stoutly bred on the dam's side, but his sire Kodiac is an influence for speed and he appeared to take after that side of his pedigree when making a winning debut in a six-furlong maiden at Doncaster in April, just needing to be kept up to his work to land the spoils by a length and a quarter. However, that first impression proved to be misleading and it wasn't until Rogue Bear stepped up to a mile later in the season that he belatedly confirmed his early promise. He spent four months on the sidelines between his second and third starts, first finishing third under a penalty in a six-furlong novice event on Town Moor and then fourth when going up to seven furlongs for his handicap debut at Ascot.

Rogue Bear was weak in the betting when tackling a mile for the first time at Nottingham in October, but he proved well suited by the increase in trip, producing a big career-best effort to win by two and a quarter lengths from Masked Identity (who advertised the strength of that form by going on to complete a four-timer) in ready fashion. Rogue Bear then did well under the circumstances to gain a share of the spoils from a 6 lb higher mark over the same course and distance three weeks later, still looking rough around the edges and forced to deliver his challenge from a long way back.

Still relatively lightly raced, Rogue Bear holds an entry in the Lincoln but is unlikely to get a run from a BHA mark of 87, so the consolation race on the same card, the Spring Mile, could be where he kicks off his four-year-old campaign instead. Wherever Rogue Bear goes in 2022, he is certainly open to more improvement and a mile and a quarter is likely to prove well within his compass when the situation demands it, too. ***Tom Clover***

Conclusion: *Proved himself useful when stepping up to a mile at the backend of last season and remains with potential heading into 2022, when he's likely to stay a mile and a quarter*

Samburu 93P

3 b.c. Kingman – Tempera (Dansili)

2021 7d* Oct 11

No fewer than 16 two-year-olds made successful debuts for John and Thady Gosden in 2021. The one who achieved most after a winning start last year was Inspiral, who ended the year unbeaten in four races after winning the Fillies' Mile on her final outing. Three days after Inspiral made her final appearance of the year, stablemate Samburu created an excellent impression with a taking debut victory in a novice at Yarmouth, looking as though he might well have a future at pattern level himself.

Samburu was among 10 newcomers in the field of 12 in which several of the top Newmarket yards were represented. The market found it hard to split the trio of Shigar, Tranquil Night and Glam de Vega, all making their debuts for William Haggas, Charlie Appleby and Roger Varian respectively. Samburu, ridden by Kieran O'Neill, was one of two newcomers for the Gosdens, both of whom were sent off at 11/1. After something of an awkward start, Samburu was soon travelling well towards the rear in just a modestly-run race before passing nearly the whole field in the last three furlongs, making good headway out wide to lead in the final furlong and then quickly asserting for a ready success. Brilliant Blue, one of the pair with some prior experience, was a length and three quarters back in second with the joint-favourites Shigar and Tranquil Night completing the frame. The latter opened his account soon after the turn of the year.

Samburu is by top-class miler Kingman whose only defeat in eight starts for John Gosden came when runner-up in the 2000 Guineas and whose best son Palace Pier was a top miler for the same stable before being retired to stud. Samburu is the first foal out of Tempera, who looked like she might be worth her place in a Guineas trial when winning a seven-furlong maiden at Leopardstown on her final two-year-old start for Dermot Weld but made a belated return at three when unable to build on that promise in just a couple of starts. Tempera's brother Set Piece, on the other hand, finished third in the Craven Stakes for Hugo Palmer before going on to show very smart form as a Grade 2 winner in the States, while her useful half-sister Alocasia (by Kingman) won a couple of listed sprints in France. Further back, this is the family of Oaks winner Reams of Verse and another filly who carried the Juddmonte colours with distinction, Midday. ***John & Thady Gosden***

Conclusion: *Plenty to like about the way he came from behind to make a winning debut on his only start last term and further progress could see him develop into a pattern-class miler*

Sea King 85p

3 br.c. Sea The Stars (Ire) – Pamona (Ire) (Duke of Marmalade (Ire))
2021 7d^5 8d^3 8m^5 t10.2s* Sep 21

Regular readers of Horses To Follow will be familiar with the typical Sir Mark Prescott two-year-old who has a trio of runs as a juvenile before stepping up in trip to make hay from a lenient mark in handicaps as a three-year-old. There's certainly better to come from Sea King, but he doesn't quite fit that stereotype. For a start, he was unusually prominent in the betting for a two-year-old debutant from his stable which has few such winners first time out, starting at 2/1 for a novice at Haydock. He proved too green to do himself justice in finishing fifth of the six runners but 10 weeks later showed the benefit of that run when stepped up to a mile for a maiden at Sandown. A steadily-run race didn't help Sea King to settle, but he showed plenty of improvement to finish third behind the Juddmonte newcomer Westover, who went on to show useful form.

Sea King improved again on his next start in the valuable Peter Willett Future Stayers' Maiden Stakes at Goodwood, run over a mile, but as the race title suggests, for horses bred to stay longer distances at three. He made the running but got involved in a battle with favourite and fellow *Fifty* member Educator from three furlongs out, leaving them both vulnerable in the closing stages as Inverness stayed on strongly to win with Sea King back in fifth. Having had three starts, Sea King might have been expected to have been put away for the winter, but he was given one more outing at Newcastle, where he was stepped up to a mile and a quarter. He relished the extra two furlongs and landed the odds in that novice in good style, scoring by three and three quarter lengths from Freedom Charter with the rest well strung out.

Sea King is sure to be suited by at least a mile and a half as there's stamina on the dam's side of his pedigree as well as from sire Sea The Stars. His dam Pamona managed to win her maiden over seven furlongs at two, but she was later suited by much longer trips, showing smart form for her other victory in a listed race at York over a mile and three quarters. Bought for 87,000 guineas as a yearling, Sea King is his dam's second winner after Rival, a fairly useful winner last season who stayed a mile and a half. Given both his pedigree and his yard, it's encouraging that Sea King has shown as much as he has already and he can only improve on that at three. ***Sir Mark Prescott Bt***

Conclusion: ***Showed plenty of ability for a yard whose stoutly-bred types invariably blossom as three-year-olds, so looks sure to have a good future over at least a mile and a half***

Second Slip (Ire) 106

5 b.g. Lope de Vega (Ire) – Arkadina (Ire) (Danehill (USA))
2021 t10.2d^3 11.9g t12.4s* t12.4s^2 t12.4d* Sep 2

England's slip catching during their latest Ashes drubbing may have been lamentable but, in stark contrast, the equine Second Slip looks like he can be relied upon.

Connections have had to be patient with Second Slip, who was unraced at two before making only three appearances as a three-year-old, his sole victory that season coming in a novice event over a mile and a quarter at Salisbury. Second Slip's four-year-old campaign didn't get off to the best of starts as he failed to justify favouritism on his reappearance at Newcastle in April, when beaten half a length into third, and then finished down the field when stepped up to a mile and a half at York's Dante Festival the following month.

However, it didn't take long for Second Slip to resume his progress. He took a big step forward when successful on his return to Gosforth Park in June, proving his stamina for a mile and a half in no uncertain terms as he forged clear in the final furlong to beat fellow *Fifty* member Hasty Sailor by four and three quarter lengths. Second Slip was unable to uphold the form when the first two met again over the same course and distance four weeks later, but he still ran at least as well in defeat, losing out by just three quarters of a length on 8 lb worse terms, and there was even better to come from him when he regained the winning thread back at Newcastle in September. Sent off the 6/4 favourite, he was always in control after being produced to lead over a furlong out, just needing to be kept up to his work to win by a length and three quarters with a bit in hand.

Second Slip was steadily progressive on the whole last season and he's got the physique (rather leggy gelding) to suggest he can do better still as he matures. Now up to a BHA mark of 96, he is likely to be a fixture in the top-end handicaps at around a mile and a half in 2022—look out for him in races such as the Duke of Edinburgh Stakes at Royal Ascot. ***James Fanshawe***

Conclusion: ***Still low mileage for his age and remains one to keep on the right side in some of the season's most valuable handicaps if picking up where he left off at the end of 2021***

Shigar (Ire) 80p

3 b.c. Farhh – Diala (Ire) (Iffraaj)

2021 7d³ 8.3s⁴ Nov 3

Close but no Shigar. That was this colt's record at two, but we're sure there are races to be won with him this year. Shigar made the frame in both his races in the autumn, showing promise behind first Samburu at Yarmouth and then Desert Crown at Nottingham, both those colts fellow members of this *Fifty*. Shigar was sent off joint-favourite to make a winning debut at Yarmouth in a novice contested mostly by other newcomers. He showed plenty of ability under a considerate ride, running green briefly when shaken up before keeping on well in the final furlong to take third near the line, two and a quarter lengths behind the impressive Samburu.

There was enough promise in that first effort for Shigar to be sent off at odds on for a maiden at Nottingham just over three weeks later, stepping up to a mile on softer ground. He didn't meet expectations, but the chances are he came up against a very good colt in Desert Crown, who could hardly have been more impressive in storming clear to win by more than five lengths. Shigar was short of room briefly two furlongs out, but that made little difference to the result as he was unable to quicken in the closing stages before coming home around six lengths behind the winner in fourth.

Shigar is a son of Godolphin's top-class Lockinge and Champion Stakes winner Farhh, who has sired good horses at a variety of trips, including the Queen Elizabeth II Stakes winner King of Change and Derby and Gold Cup runner-up Dee Ex Bee. Shigar's dam Diala raced for the same connections and made a big enough impression in winning her maiden at Newmarket on her final two-year-old start to contest the 1000 Guineas on her return the following season. She finished down the field there and ended the season in handicaps without adding to her tally but did show that she stayed a mile. Diala has done well at stud, producing three winners to date, including the fairly useful Constanta, who won over Wolverhampton's extended nine furlongs last season.

However, her best foal so far was smart miler Skardu, who won the Craven Stakes for William Haggas and Abdulla Al Khalifa before finishing third in the 2000 Guineas. Shigar looks potentially his dam's best foal since, and he too will prove fully effective over a mile. ***William Haggas***

Conclusion: *Half-brother to connections' smart miler Skardu and offered plenty to work on behind a couple of promising sorts in the autumn, so well up to winning races this season*

Sisters In The Sky 83

3 ch.c. Showcasing – Sunny York (Ire) (Vale of York (Ire))

2021 6.1m^{3} 6g^{5} 6s* 6m^{5} 5m^{6} Sep 24

Sisters In The Sky might have won only one of his five starts at two, but there are grounds for thinking more races will be coming his way this year. His only win came in a maiden, but connections found a good one for him to win as it came at Glorious Goodwood and was a valuable race of its type worth more than £13,000 on offer to the winner. Sisters In The Sky ran out a ready winner by a length from newcomer Monet's Sunrise after taking the lead under Hollie Doyle inside the last two furlongs, making his experience count. The same race had been won the year before by Alkumait, who went on to win the Mill Reef Stakes, but the latest renewal, run on soft ground, wasn't that strong a contest for the money on offer.

Sisters In The Sky gets off the mark at Goodwood

Sisters In The Sky ran twice in novices before Goodwood, showing some ability to finish third on his debut at Chester before fading into fifth after making much of the running at Newbury. That proved to be better form than it looked at the time, with the winner Bosh going close in a valuable sales race in Ireland and runner-up American Star contesting pattern races later in the season. After his win at Goodwood, Sisters In The Sky went on to the Ebor Festival where he shaped well on his nursery debut in a 20-runner contest which proved strong form. On much firmer ground than at Goodwood, he showed bags of speed from a favourable low draw, taking the lead over two furlongs out and headed only inside the last before finishing around two lengths behind winner Flaming Rib (who went to complete a four-timer in a listed race) in fifth.

Raced at six furlongs to that point, Sisters In The Sky had shown enough pace to suggest a try at the minimum trip was well worth a shot and he was made joint-favourite for another good-quality nursery at Haydock in September. However, a line can be put through that attempt as things went wrong for him right from the off when he reared leaving the stalls and never got into it trying to challenge widest of all. He's much better judged on the good impression he'd made at York and looks up to winning sprint handicaps. Sisters In The Sky has the build of a sprinter—he's a compact colt—and is bred for speed, too, by the Gimcrack winner Showcasing out of a mare who ran her best race when making a winning debut at two over five furlongs. ***Roger Teal***

Conclusion: ***Showed potential for sprint handicaps last year, displaying plenty of speed in a competitive nursery at York after getting off the mark at Goodwood and easily forgiven his final start***

Symbol of Light 104p

3 b.g. Shamardal (USA) – Pure Diamond (Street Cry (Ire))

2021 8m³ t8.6s* t8.6s* :: 2022 t8.1g* Jan 27

An era ended at Southwell last August when the Nottinghamshire track staged its final meeting on fibresand which had been the all-weather surface there since 1989. Fibresand was more testing in nature than the other all-weather surfaces, something which suited some horses who became true track specialists, none more so than the David Chapman-trained Tempering who won 22 races there in the 1990s. It wasn't every horse's, or punter's, cup of tea, however, and Southwell's switch to tapeta, already in use at Newcastle and Wolverhampton, was welcomed as a positive move overall. There has already been some better-quality racing since the new surface came into use last December; Charlie Appleby, for example, had his first-ever runners at Southwell after the change in surface and three winners for Godolphin soon followed in January.

One of those was Symbol of Light, who carried top weight to victory in a three-year-old handicap over a mile, Adam Kirby dictating a slow pace before kicking on early in the straight and asserting in the final furlong. That was a useful effort from Symbol of Light, who was completing a hat-trick of odds-on victories on the all-weather. He had won a couple of novices at Wolverhampton late last year, easily winning the first of them and then following up readily under a penalty. That followed his debut in a Newmarket maiden earlier in the autumn where he gradually got the hang of things as the race progressed and wasn't given too hard an introduction in finishing third to Subastar and just in front of another member of the *Fifty*, Magisterial.

Symbol of Light had already been gelded before his debut and, while he might not end up figuring among the best of his stable's talented team of three-year-olds, he's open to further improvement nonetheless, including over longer trips than he's tackled so far. His useful dam Pure Diamond also began her career successfully on the all-weather, winning twice over a mile at Kempton as a two-year-old, and she went on to win a listed race over seven furlongs on turf at Meydan as a three-year-old. The best of her siblings was Godolphin's Elite Army, another who started out with a win on the all-weather before becoming a smart mile and a half performer on turf, with his wins including the King George V Stakes at Royal Ascot. ***Charlie Appleby***

Conclusion: ***Three-time all-weather winner for Godolphin who still has improvement in him, particularly when tried over further than a mile***

Tiempo Star 88

3 b.g. Time Test – Tanaasub (Ire) (Lope de Vega (Ire))

2021 7m 7m³ 8.5m² p8g* Oct 4

Time Test showed high-class form at up to a mile and a quarter in the colours of the late Khalid Abdullah, with four of his six wins in the care of Roger Charlton coming in pattern company; the Tercentenary Stakes at Royal Ascot and Joel Stakes at Newmarket at three, and the Brigadier Gerard Stakes at Sandown and York Stakes at four. He also raced in the States at five before beginning his stallion career at the National Stud in 2018. Time Test had his first crop of two-year-olds last season, and such was their promise that it resulted in his fee being raised from £8,500 to £15,000 this year. His leading performers included the Irish filly Sunset Shiraz, third in the Moyglare Stud Stakes, the Dick Poole Fillies' Stakes winner Romantic Time and the listed winner Tardis, while Rocchigiani was a Group 3 winner in Germany. Tiempo Star wasn't tried at that sort of level, but he was one of Time Test's better two-year-olds and ended the season as another of his sire's winners.

There wasn't much immediate sign of promise on Tiempo Star's debut at Sandown in July, but he showed more ability when third to Tatsumaki in a novice at Newmarket next time, the useful winner ending up unbeaten in three starts. Stepped up to the extended mile at Epsom, Tiempo Star took another step forward when going down narrowly in a three-runner maiden won by the Godolphin gelding New Mission, tackling the eventual winner over a furlong out and keeping on despite that rival carrying him right in the closing stages. For his final start in October, Tiempo Star was sent off favourite for his nursery debut, which was also his first start on the all-weather, at Lingfield. He duly proved himself a progressive sort in coming out narrowly on top and was value for a bit more than his short-head margin of victory as he came from off the pace to peg back a couple of more prominently-ridden rivals, Sharp Combo and Incumbent, in the shadow of the post.

Tiempo Star will begin his three-year-old campaign on a BHA mark of 83, only 4 lb higher than when winning at Lingfield, and the way he progressed at two suggests there should be more handicaps to be won with him having been gelded over the winter. Tiempo Star fetched only 10,000 guineas as a foal but joined current connections for 42,000 guineas earlier in 2021. His dam was a sprinter in keeping with quite a speedy family on the whole, so Tiempo Star isn't sure to stay much beyond a mile himself. ***Ralph Beckett***

Conclusion: *Progressed with each run to conclude two-year-old season with a successful nursery debut and more handicaps should come his way at three*

Trojan Horse (Ire) 83p

3 ch.c. Ulysses (Ire) – Guardia (Ger) (Monsun (Ger))
2021 7.9s^3 9d* Oct 25

Back in 1993, Mark Johnston won a nine-furlong maiden at Redcar with a flashy chestnut two-year-old named Double Trigger, whose 10-length victory on his debut proved to be the first of 14 victories in a famous staying career during which he won a Gold Cup along with three Goodwood Cups and three Doncaster Cups. Double Trigger, who died aged 29 in 2020, now has a novice for two-year-olds named after him over the same course and distance where it all began for him. The latest renewal of that contest in October was won by another chestnut colt, not only from the Johnston yard but also part-owned by Ron Huggins, the owner of Double Trigger.

The Redcar race was Trojan Horse's second start after he'd made a promising debut at York earlier in the month. In a novice contested mostly by newcomers, Trojan Horse plugged on for third behind Luna Dorada and Gin O'Clock who pulled clear. He clearly appreciated the extra furlong at Redcar where Joe Fanning sent him for home soon after leading under three furlongs out. He was always holding on from there as he beat the William Haggas-trained favourite Three Start by a length and three quarters with the pair clear of the rest.

Johnston has said that the ability of a horse's dam 'is the be all and end all as far as I'm concerned' when it comes to buying yearlings. With a Timeform rating of 109, Trojan Horse's dam Guardia therefore easily exceeded Johnston's 'quality control' mark of 90. Guardia's two wins in Germany and France came at around a mile and a quarter, while her smart sister Guadalupe won the Oaks d'Italia and was second in the Yorkshire Oaks and her brother Getaway, now a leading sire of jumpers, was a high-class performer at up to 15 furlongs in France and Germany. No less significantly for Johnston, this is also the family of another of his best stayers, Royal Rebel, whose wins included two Gold Cups and a Goodwood Cup. The well-named Trojan Horse also comes from the promising first crop of the Eclipse and Juddmonte International winner Ulysses. ***Charlie & Mark Johnston***

Conclusion: *Off the mark in a race named after Double Trigger for the same connections as that very smart stayer, and pedigree strongly suggests he'll come into his own over longer trips this year*

Tuddenham Green 73p

3 b.g. Nathaniel (Ire) – Social Media (New Approach (Ire))

2021 7m p8s[6] p8g[4] Nov 30

It would be no surprise to see Tuddenham Green running over hurdles one day. After all, he's a gelding, he's trained by Alan King and he runs in the 'double green' colours of Simon Munir and Isaac Souede. While his trainer is no stranger to success on the Flat as well these days, his owners remain much more associated with the jumping game, with Sceau Royal continuing to do them proud over both hurdles and fences for the King yard. Whatever the longer-term plan for Tuddenham Green might be over jumps, though, there should be races to be won with him first on the Flat.

Tuddenham Green progressed with each run at two, enough to be interesting when stepping up in trip in handicaps. Admittedly, there wasn't much encouragement from his debut over seven furlongs at Haydock in June when he trailed throughout after a very slow start, but, after a break of five months, there was much more to like about his two runs over a mile on the all-weather in November. He kept on from the rear, despite being short of room in the final furlong, to finish sixth in a bunched finish to a novice at Kempton won by the filly Rochebrune, and then fared best of those with experience when fourth in a maiden at Lingfield which turned out to be a stronger contest. Slowly away again, Tuddenham Green wasn't given too hard a race in the end after making some headway under pressure from midfield entering the straight and was beaten just over three lengths at the line. Both the first two, Yonafis and Al Marmar, went on to win their next starts, showing fairly useful form.

Tuddenham Green was bought for 24,000 guineas as a yearling and is by Enable's sire Nathaniel, who has a growing reputation as a sire of jumpers these days, another reason for thinking that might be where Tuddenham Green's future lies—Nathaniel's daughter Concertista has already carried the 'double green' colours to success at the Cheltenham Festival. There's plenty of stamina in Tuddenham Green's family as his dam Social Media gained her only win in a two-mile handicap at Wolverhampton. She was a half-sister to the Lancashire Oaks winner Horseplay (and to Devilment, a smart hurdler) and out of the useful filly Mischief Making, who was runner-up in the Sagaro Stakes over two miles. Coincidentally, the runner-up in Tuddenham Green's last race, Al Marmar, is a half-brother to his grandam. ***Alan King***

Conclusion: *Went the right way in his three starts last year and is very much bred to be suited by longer distances, so he's one to note in handicaps*

Twilight Calls 103

4 b.g. Twilight Son – Zawiyah (Invincible Spirit (Ire))

2021 6g* 6g² 5m* 5d⁴ 5.4m⁶ Aug 18

Twilight Calls won twice last season and ran well on his other three starts, going off favourite every time, yet the overall impression he created was that of a horse for whom the penny hadn't quite yet dropped and it could be that another winter on his back, plus a gelding operation, will be the making of him. If that's the case he's a well-handicapped sprinter with smart potential for a trainer in Henry Candy who has long excelled with such types.

The key feature of virtually all of Twilight Calls's runs so far has been a high cruising speed, which was never more in evidence than for his win over five furlongs at Newmarket's July meeting, when he readily got the better of subsequent dual winner King of Stars with the pair clear of the rest. Twilight Calls wasn't seen to best effect when an unlucky-in-running fourth from well off the pace (behind fellow *Fifty* member Whenthedealinsdone) over the same trip at Goodwood later that month, and while there were fewer excuses when he was only sixth in a hot race at York's Ebor Festival on his final outing, he once again caught the eye by going on the bridle for longer than almost anything else.

It wouldn't be a surprise if it was by design that Twilight Calls didn't run again last season, and Candy's trademark patient approach is one that regularly pays dividends. Indeed, he expertly developed both Twilight Calls's sire Twilight Son and grandsire Kyllachy from handicappers into Group 1 winners. Clearly, it's asking a lot for that family tradition to continue, but it'll be a big surprise if Twilight Calls doesn't prove a fair bit better than a BHA mark of 94 and, if things really go to plan, it's not out of the question he could make the jump to a higher level. ***Henry Candy***

Twilight Calls (No. 13, red silks with blue cap) is one to follow in sprint handicaps

Conclusion: *Lightly raced sort who quickly reached a useful level last season and should have even more to offer as a four-year-old, representing a yard that has excelled with similar types in the past*

Ville de Grace 113p

4 b.f. Le Havre (Ire) – Archangel Gabriel (USA) (Arch (USA))

2021 7g5 7.9g 8g3 10.1g* 10d* Oct 8

Last season's Dubai Duty Free Stakes at Newbury, better known as the Fred Darling, turned out to be a rich source of winners. It might not have lived up to its traditional billing as a 1000 Guineas trial—the first three all ran at Newmarket without reaching the frame—but winner Alcohol Free, who was fifth in the 1000 Guineas, turned out to be one of the leading fillies of her generation, winning the Coronation Stakes and Sussex Stakes. She wasn't the only good horse to come out of the huge field of 17. Five of the beaten fillies at Newbury ended the year with smart Timeform ratings of between 111 and 115, including the trio of huge-priced outsiders who finished third, fourth and fifth, Vadream, Primo Bacio and Ville de Grace. Vadream was the speediest of the three, later winning the Group 3 Bengough Stakes over six furlongs at Ascot,

Primo Bacio ran in some of the top fillies' races at a mile, while it took a step up to a mile and a quarter at the end of the season for Ville de Grace to show her true worth.

Ville de Grace had evidently been showing a fair amount of speed at two as her two starts that year were both over six furlongs and she made a winning debut at Kempton. After a keeping-on fifth on her reappearance in the Fred Darling, Ville de Grace beat only one home in a listed race at York won by Primo Bacio on her next start, but she fared better after a three-month break, returning in August to finish a never-nearer third behind the 1000 Guineas runner-up Saffron Beach in the Atalanta Stakes at Sandown. Ville de Grace kept on well on her second attempt at a mile, but it was the step up to a mile and a quarter which brought about marked improvement in a listed race for fillies at Yarmouth the following month.

She came home three lengths clear of consistent older rival Freyja, with favourite Sweet Believer back in third, and when the first three met again in the Group 3 Pride Stakes at Newmarket in October, Ville de Grace fared much the best of them in following up in good style, the way she moved through the race before quickening to the front suggesting that there's further improvement to come from her. It looked form worth viewing positively, too, as Ville de Grace beat Lilac Road, a listed winner herself last time out, by half a length, the pair coming a little way clear of the rest. ***Sir Michael Stoute***

Conclusion: *Only really started to come into her own when tackling a mile and a quarter in the autumn and looks capable of winning more good fillies' races at four*

Whenthedealinsdone 110

4 b.g. Dark Angel (Ire) – Maureen (Ire) (Holy Roman Emperor (Ire))
2021 6m⁴ 6s 5.1m* 6m⁶ 5d* 5.4m 5.6d⁵ Sep 11

2021 was a landmark year for trainer Roger Teal. Not only did he double his best previous tally of winners in a season, but Oxted also provided the stable with further Group 1 success in the King's Stand Stakes at Royal Ascot. Oxted announced himself as a sprinter potentially destined for the top when landing the Portland Handicap at Doncaster as a three-year-old, and while his stable-companion Whenthedealinsdone only managed fifth when trying to emulate that feat last year, the way he shaped that day, not to mention his overall profile, leaves no doubt that he's a sprint handicapper to have on side in 2022.

Whenthedealinsdone was gelded before his third start of last season and it was then that he proved himself well treated, first-time cheekpieces also putting an extra edge on him for his win in a five-furlong handicap at Windsor in June. Whenthedealinsdone also ran a fine race when sixth (second in the disadvantaged group) in a big field over a furlong further at Newmarket's July meeting next time, but he seemed especially well suited by dropping back in distance when landing a competitive event at Goodwood later that month, keeping going well to land the spoils by a length and a half. He wasn't quite so good on his first try against older horses at York's Ebor Festival afterwards, albeit beaten less than four lengths, but it didn't take him long to bounce back as he signed off with that fifth in the Portland. That run was even better than the bare result—he entered the final furlong upsides, looking no worse than third best—and perhaps the extended distance of the Portland found him out late on.

The next-time wins of the first two, Hurricane Ivor and Boundless Power (who is also included in the *Fifty*), underline the strength of that form, anyway, and there's no doubt that Whenthedealinsdone embarks on his four-year-old campaign well treated from the same mark as for that effort. What's more, he's lightly raced enough to think there'll be more progress to come, and it'll be a surprise if he doesn't win a few more handicaps in 2022, maybe even on his way to something better. ***Roger Teal***

Conclusion: *Shaped well when fifth in a good edition of the Portland and he may have more to offer when dropped back to a bare five furlongs*

David Johnson (**Whenthedealinsdone:**): *"The Portland proved a good piece of sprint handicap form last year. The first two both won their next starts and, having shaped as well as that pair, Whenthedealinsdone looks set to give it a further boost in 2022. Though a six-furlong winner at two, he's got faster as well as better as he's matured, with both wins last year coming at the minimum trip, and it was the extended distance of the Portland rather than his mark which found him out there. I think he can win a decent handicap before perhaps joining his stablemate Oxted in pattern company."*

Witch Hunter (Fr) 104

3 b.c. Siyouni (Fr) – Sorciere (Ire) (Orpen (USA))

2021 6g^{2} 6s^{3} 6s^{2} Oct 9

Not many maidens have a Timeform rating in excess of 100 and those that do don't tend to remain maidens for long. Hopefully, that will be the case with Witch Hunter, who is still seeking his first win but went close in all three of his starts last year. It was well into September before Witch Hunter made his debut and, while he didn't quite reward the strong support which made him the 7/4 favourite for the maiden at Newbury, he made a promising start, edging ahead inside the final furlong but headed in the last 50 yards by another of the newcomers, Deodar, who beat him a neck.

Witch Hunter is evidently held in some regard as he was also entered in a Group 3 at the time of his debut and, instead of taking the easier option of another maiden, for his second start he contested a conditions race at Salisbury and was unlucky not to win it. In a tight finish, Witch Hunter came off third-best, beaten a short head and a neck behind favourite Ribhi and Atheby. Crucially, he only saw daylight close home after having no room when making headway in the final furlong, still appearing to have a bit left to give at the line. Witch Hunter looked a banker to get off the mark in maiden or novice company at the third attempt, but his sights were raised again for his final start. Despite not having won a race, Witch Hunter had better form claims than many in the listed Rockingham Stakes at York, and he duly ran well again in defeat, improving further and finding only the filly Canonized, the pick on form, three quarters of a length too strong.

The reputation of Witch Hunter's sire Siyouni has never been higher after the exploits of his son St Mark's Basilica last year which came soon after another of his best horses, Sottsass, won the Arc in 2020. Another of Siyouni's better horses was Straight Right, who proved smart at up to a mile for Andrew Balding and comes from the same family as Witch Hunter, who was a £125,000 breeze-up purchase last year. His dam, Sorciere, was a useful two-year-old sprinter in France, beating the future 1000 Guineas winner Special Duty on her debut and later winning the Group 3 Prix d'Arenberg at Chantilly. Sorciere has produced three winners abroad to date, including French listed winner Medley Chic, a winner at up to ten and a half furlongs. It looks only a matter of time before Witch Hunter, a useful-looking colt, becomes her fourth, and potentially best, winner. Proven on soft ground, he'll stay seven furlongs. ***Richard Hannon***

Conclusion: *Placed in all three of his starts last year, beaten less than a length each time, and shouldn't be long losing his maiden tag before progressing further*

Wootton'sun (Fr) 77p

3 b.c. Wootton Bassett – Sous Le Soleil (USA) (Tizway (USA))

2021 6g^{6} 7.8m^{4} 7.2m^{3} 7.9s^{5} Oct 9

When Richard Fahey debuted a two-year-old son of Iffraaj at Ayr in June 2010, he could hardly have imagined that 11 years later he'd be training a son of the same horse who would by then have become one of Europe's most sought-after stallions. Wootton Bassett not only made a winning debut at Ayr but went unbeaten in five starts as a two-year-old, culminating in a first Group 1 victory for his trainer, and jockey Paul Hanagan, in the Prix Jean-Luc Lagardere at Longchamp. Wootton Bassett failed to cut much ice in Group 1 company at three but, as the winner of France's top race for two-year-olds, he had earned a place at stud, albeit at a fee of just €6,000 at the Head family's Haras d'Etreham in Normandy. However, just as he did as a racehorse, Wootton Bassett has worked his way up from humble beginnings to the top of the tree as a stallion. Siring Almanzor, Timeform's Horse of the Year in 2016, from a first crop of just 23 foals, was a massive boost to Wootton Bassett's stud career. Other good horses followed and in 2020, in a deal costing millions, he was transferred to Coolmore Stud in Ireland where he now stands as the most expensive stallion on their roster at €150,000.

Wootton'sun might be a son of Wootton Bassett, but he was a very different two-year-old from his sire. Even on his fourth and final start last year in a competitive nursery at York, Wootton'sun still looked a work in progress, racing too freely before finishing a creditable fifth behind Oh Herberts Reign. It's the expectation that he'll make a much better three-year-old once he figures things out fully that makes him a good candidate for the *Fifty*. Wootton'sun progressed in his three novice races before his nursery debut at York. He never threatened first time out over six furlongs at Redcar and wasn't given too hard a time either when fourth at Carlisle, but he showed more on his third start in quite a competitive race at Ayr's September meeting when keeping on well to take third on the post, a length and a half behind winner Green Team.

At 100,000 guineas, Wootton'sun cost more than twice what his sire had fetched as a yearling. He's the first foal of Sous Le Soleil, a winner over a mile and a half, and over hurdles, in France, while his German grandam Que Belle was a very smart filly, considered good enough to contest the Arc after winning both the fillies' classics in her own country. All that suggests Wootton'sun will be well suited by distances in excess of a mile this year. ***Richard Fahey***

Conclusion: *Still learning at two but cost plenty and shapes as though handicaps over a mile and a quarter or more will come his way when everything falls into place*

SECTION 2

Buckaroo **107p**

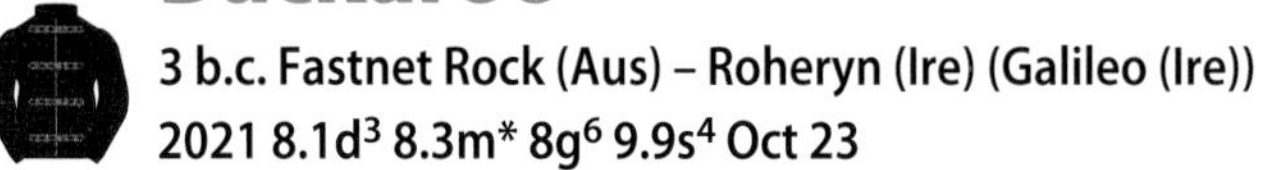

3 b.c. Fastnet Rock (Aus) – Roheryn (Ire) (Galileo (Ire))
2021 8.1d^{3} 8.3m* 8g^{6} 9.9s^{4} Oct 23

'Put on a shovel, try a pick, if it's too heavy the mule will kick!' Buckaroo was a game which kept generations of children from the 1970s onwards—as well as Father Dougal in the Channel 4 comedy Father Ted—entertained by trying to place as many items as possible on the back of the said plastic mule before they were bucked off. Fortunately for his jockeys, Qatar Racing's colt of the same name has shown no such similar antics and looks a potentially smart staying three-year-old for Joseph O'Brien's stable.

Buckaroo made an eye-catching debut in a maiden at Killarney in July when nearest at the finish to take third after a slow start and, later in the month at the Galway Festival, he confirmed that promise when justifying even-money favouritism in a similar event. That particular race has been farmed by Aidan O'Brien in recent seasons, but on this occasion his runner Stone Age went down by a neck as the pair finished clear. Stone Age finished in front of Buckaroo in both their subsequent meetings, though Buckaroo kept improving and shaped well on both occasions. They next met in the Group 2 KPMG Champions Juvenile Stakes at Leopardstown which turned into a messy contest, with Atomic Jones getting the better of Stone Age by a head in a bunched finish, while Buckaroo was one of those who wasn't seen to best effect after not getting the best of runs in the straight before keeping on for a close sixth. On his final start, Buckaroo was sent to France for the Criterium de Saint-Cloud over a mile and a quarter on soft ground, a serious test of stamina for two-year-olds. Buckaroo shaped like a real stayer, still having plenty to do in rear turning for home but closing all the way to the line for fourth, just under three lengths behind the British-trained winner El Bodegon, who benefited from an enterprising ride in front to hold on from the staying-on Stone Age.

Buckaroo's sire Fastnet Rock has had good winners at a variety of trips, including Torcedor who was a very smart stayer. His dam Roheryn was a useful filly by Galileo who won a listed race at Leopardstown over a mile and a half and stayed a mile and three quarters. Roheryn is also the dam of Thousand Oaks, a mile and a half winner at Newmarket last year who shaped as though she'd be suited by longer trips, and of the fairly useful hurdler Kihavah. Buckaroo looks sure to be suited by at least a mile and a half himself. ***Joseph O'Brien***

Conclusion: *Improved with each run at two and has the makings of a smart staying three-year-old after signing off with a promising run in a Group 1*

Crystal Black (Ire) 98

4 b.g. Teofilo (Ire) – She's Our Mark (Ishiguru (USA))
2021 8d 9.4g* 6d 8g^{6} 10g^{3} Sep 12

The unexposed Crystal Black showed useful form in his first season of racing as a three-year-old and he looks the type who'll improve further and win more races at four. He was sent off at 25/1 for his debut in a big field of maidens at Leopardstown in May and hinted at ability in mid-division throughout. It was a couple of months before Crystal Black was seen out again and he showed a good deal of improvement to win a similar event at Ballinrobe, stepping up from a mile to an extended nine furlongs. In staying on to lead in the final 50 yards for a comfortable three-length success, Crystal Black gave the impression he'd benefitted from the step up in trip and his jockey Oisin Orr confirmed as much afterwards, saying 'for most of the way around here he didn't travel but he hit the line well…he stays well and I think he will get a bit further too.'

It was a surprise, therefore, when Crystal Black made his handicap debut at the Curragh next time over six furlongs. There's nothing whatsoever about Crystal Black to suggest he's a sprinter and, sure enough, he was only able to make some late headway from the rear to finish ninth of the 15 runners. That ploy didn't result in any leniency from the handicapper, either, as he ran off the same mark back at the Curragh later in August in the Irish Cambridgeshire. Visored for the first time, and back at a more suitable trip of a mile, he ran his best race to that point, staying on for sixth of the 27 runners behind the decisive winner Bopedro. Crystal Black fared better still in another competitive handicap at the Curragh, the 'Northfields' which is a valuable mile and a quarter event run on Irish Champions weekend. It had been won the year before by Sonnyboyliston, who returned to win the Irish St Leger on the same card 12 months later having won the Ebor on his previous start. Visored again, Crystal Black had the outside draw in the 23-runner field and took a keen hold out wide but quickened to lead entering the final furlong before going down by a pair of necks to another unexposed three-year-old Max Mayhem and the thriving four-year-old filly Pineapple Express.

Crystal Black is his dam's fourth winner, the other three being by sires that are much more of an influence for speed than his own sire Teofilo. Their dam She's Our Mark was a grand mare, both smart and versatile trip-wise, and the fact that she won up to a mile and a half in the Group 3 Give Thanks Stakes suggests Crystal Black might stay that far himself. ***Dermot Weld***

Conclusion: *Starts 2022 as an unexposed four-year-old handicapper with potential for further improvement at beyond a mile*

Ever Present (Ire) 112

6 b. or br.g. Elusive Pimpernel (USA) – Persian Memories (Ire) (Indian Ridge)
2021 15m* 15g* 16g² 12.8g* Sep 11

Bumpers are mainly intended to be a launch-pad for a jumping career, of course, but occasionally they can throw up a horse who goes on to excel on the Flat instead and Ever Present looks just such an animal. Training top jumpers or Flat horses all comes alike to Jessica Harrington and she started off Ever Present—who is bred more for the Flat but was presumably too backward as a youngster—as a four-year-old in a bumper for newcomers at Punchestown in October 2020. Sent off at 25/1 in a contest where inevitably the likes of Gordon Elliott and Willie Mullins had better-fancied runners, Ever Present defied those big odds to make a successful debut, but he found life tougher when contesting better-quality contests in his three remaining bumpers which were won respectively by Sir Gerhard, Kilcruit and Dysart Dynamo, all of whom have since made a name for themselves over hurdles.

Ever Present, on the other hand, had his attentions switched to the Flat in the summer of 2021 and won his first two starts in that sphere in 'Q.R.' or amateur contests. That enabled Ever Present's partnership with his teenage bumper pilot Mikey McGuane to be maintained; his Punchestown victory had been the 16-year-old's first winner on just his second ride under Rules. Ever Present made a good impression on his Flat debut, forging clear for a six-length win in a maiden at Leopardstown in June, and he then showed a good turn of foot to follow up in a minor event over the same course and distance the following month.

Shane Foley took over in the saddle for Ever Present's last two starts in handicaps and he showed plenty of improvement in both. Outstayed over two miles when going down to the mare Dinard Rose, who was in receipt of plenty of weight, at the Curragh next time, he then got his head back in front when dropped in trip for the Petingo Handicap, a valuable and competitive contest back at Leopardstown on Irish Champions weekend. Under joint top-weight of 10-0, Ever Present put up a smart effort over the extended mile and a half trip, finding plenty when asked for his effort and staying on to lead close home for a length and a half victory over another unexposed type in Ciel d'Afrique. As one who looks as though he'll prove best at short of two miles on the Flat, Ever Present could be an ideal type for the Ebor this season, a race his trainer indicated he'd be aimed at, though he'd also be worth his place in listed company at least. ***Jessica Harrington***

Conclusion: *Graduate from bumpers who soon showed smart form in handicap company when switched to the Flat and remains unexposed with the Ebor said to be the target*

History (Ire) 96p

3 b.f. Galileo (Ire) – Prize Exhibit (Showcasing)
2021 7d² 7.5g² 8d* Sep 18

Ballydoyle had wretched luck with a couple of its best three-year-old fillies of 2021. Snowfall ran away with the Oaks at Epsom by a record margin before following up in the Irish and Yorkshire Oaks, and she was all set to be covered by St Mark's Basilica this spring when having to be put down in January after sustaining an injury in her box. That followed the loss of stablemate Santa Barbara, who didn't live up to her huge reputation in the fillies' classics earlier in the year but went on to win a couple of Grade 1 contests in the States before she too succumbed to a pelvic injury. Hopefully, fate will be kinder to History, who could make into a classic contender herself if continuing to go the right way in the spring.

History found only the Ger Lyons fillies Cairde Go Deo and Panama Red too strong on her first couple of starts at the Curragh and Tipperary, but there was no disgrace in that, with the former starting favourite for the Moyglare Stud Stakes next time and the latter going on to win in listed company. History improved with each run and got

History is from the family of the top-class miler Mohaather

off the mark at the third attempt when stepping up to a mile in a maiden at Gowran in September. She travelled well close to the pace and the result was never really in doubt after she was produced to lead entering the final two furlongs, ultimately beating the Joseph O'Brien-trained newcomer Clemmie C by two and a half lengths in ready fashion.

Another loss which must have hit History's connections hard last year was that of her sire Galileo, who died at the age of 23. History had cost 2.8 million guineas when going through the ring at Tattersalls as a yearling which was some measure of Galileo's standing as a stallion, though an even more expensive purchase by the Coolmore team was another Galileo filly, a sister to their Group 1 winners Japan and Mogul, who fetched 3.4 million. Now named Skylark, she didn't race at two. History's price tag was only partly down to her sire, though, as her female family became a lot more attractive in the months leading up to her sale thanks to the exploits of her dam's brother Mohaather, who was a most impressive winner of the Sussex Stakes. History's dam Prize Exhibit began her career at two with Jamie Osborne before developing into a smart filly across the Atlantic where she won four graded stakes at up to a mile. She was a quirky sort who wore headgear for most of her starts. History will presumably start off at a mile in the spring, but her sire always gives hope for his offspring staying longer trips. ***Aidan O'Brien***

Conclusion: *Improved with each run at two and, given her pedigree and connections, there should be more to come*

Masen 120

4 b.g. Kingman – Continental Drift (USA) (Smart Strike (CAN))
2021 8.1g^2 7.2g* 7g* Oct 23

Ger Lyons began the 2021 edition of Irish Champions Weekend in terrific fashion, notably winning half of the eight races on the opening afternoon at Leopardstown, including the Group 2 Champions Juvenile Stakes with Atomic Jones. However, in performance terms, the best was saved for last as Masen ran out a decisive winner of the closing handicap over seven furlongs. In running to a Timeform rating of 113 (with 3 lb extra awarded for his superiority), he put up the best winning effort in the race since Kelinni in 2015, a performance which, in theory, would have had him in the frame in the Group 2 Park Stakes run over the same trip at Doncaster earlier in the day.

That run was a real coming-of-age moment for Masen, who had often raced too freely to show his true potential earlier in his career. Gelded at the end of his juvenile season, Masen again pulled too hard when returning in a listed race over a mile at Killarney in August, but the application of a hood seemingly acted as the catalyst for what was a much-improved display at Leopardstown. Never far off the pace, Masen settled much better than previously and hit the front travelling well at the two-furlong marker. He was clear with a furlong to run and looked to have a bit in hand at line despite the best efforts of the placed pair who finished strongly to reduce the deficit to just half a length.

Irish Champions Weekend may be the pinnacle for some, but for Masen it proved merely a springboard as six weeks later he was back at the Dublin track when dominating 15 rivals in a listed race. Allowed his head in front, he set a gallop that proved far too hot for the majority, ultimately winning by two and a quarter lengths and again looking likely to win by further for a long way before his advantage was reduced late on. A Timeform rating of 120 puts him in the very smart bracket, while a timefigure on the day of 106—plus a sectional uplift of 20 lb (such was the fierce pace he set—suggests there is every chance he can rate higher again at four.

All three of Masen's victories have come on good ground over seven furlongs at Leopardstown, but his run style suggests good to firm ought to be no problem for him. There is little doubt he has the ability to make an impact at an even higher level and races such as the Gladness Stakes, a Group 3 run over seven furlongs at the Curragh in April, are likely to feature highly on his agenda. Given his enthusiastic nature, he will probably have no problem with a stiff six furlongs if the situation demands it, too. ***Ger Lyons***

Conclusion: *Much improved on his final two starts at three and looks well up to winning group races this year if continuing to channel his energy in the right direction*

Rhea Moon (Ire) 88p

3 b.f. Starspangledbanner (Aus) – Callisto Star (Ire) (Fastnet Rock (Aus))
2021 p6g^3 6s^2 Aug 21

Rhea Moon heads into the new season as a maiden, but that is unlikely to remain the case for long based on how much promise she showed in two starts last year. Well backed and sent off at 5/2 when making her debut at Dundalk in August, Rhea Moon duly shaped with plenty promise despite having to settle for third, leaving the impression she would have won had a slow start not resulted in her being held up in a race run at a modest tempo. Rhea Moon still had plenty on her plate as the field entered the straight, but she finished with a flourish, clocking a notable sectional time to pass the post just a length behind the winner.

Rhea Moon looked sure to progress for that experience and, turned out at the Curragh six days later, she duly posted an improved effort to fill the runner-up spot behind a rival who subsequently bolted up in a listed race. Time has shown that Rhea Moon probably had little chance against Straight Answer—a devastating five-and-a-half-length winner of the Blenheim Stakes on his next outing—but her chance wasn't helped by allowing that rival to secure first run in the centre of the course. She again impressed with how powerfully she saw out her race, showing more than enough to suggest that she has a bigger effort in the locker when everything falls right.

Rhea Moon is by a champion sprinter in Starspangledbanner, but her unraced dam, Callisto Star, is out of a daughter of Galileo who won three times over a mile and a half. That offers hope that Rhea Moon will stay further than six furlongs, the only distance she tackled when strong at the finish in both starts as a juvenile. ***Ken Condon***

Conclusion: *Offered plenty to work on in two starts last season and looks a banker for a maiden at least after chasing home a pattern performer at the Curragh*

Safari Quest (Ire) 90

4 b.g. Australia – Lucy Diamonds (Ire) (Orpen (USA))
2021 10d3 10d2 12.7g 11.2g4 9.5g* Sep 1

It took the well-bred Safari Quest six attempts to get off the mark, but an authoritative success in a maiden at Gowran Park on his final start of the campaign suggests he is one to note for a valuable handicap in 2022. He had shown promise earlier in the season, bumping into some useful sorts when third at Leopardstown in April and runner-up at Navan in May, but it all came together with a much-improved display at Gowran, resulting in a two-length victory in a race which has worked out well (the second and the third have both won since). The application of a tongue tie for the first time may have aided his cause, though it's probably also the case that Safari Quest is still maturing and can kick on again this season.

Safari Quest, a son of Australia, is a brother to Roca Roma, a mare who showed useful form for Ger Lyons as a four-year-old during the latest season. She produced a career-best effort when defying a mark of 97 to win a handicap at Killarney in July before finding only the smart Pearls Galore too strong in a Group 3 at Tipperary. Safari Quest is also a half-brother to Roca Rojo, a mare who won a Group 2 in America as a five-year-old, while his most illustrious sibling, Beauty Flame, proved to be a big money-spinner in Hong Kong and produced his best Timeform rating of 119 as a six-year-old. The family's record offers encouragement that Safari Quest can pick up where he left off and progress during 2022. A mark of 84 should certainly be within his range. ***Ger Lyons***

Conclusion: *Well-bred sort who ended last season with a decisive success in a maiden which has worked out well and should make hay in handicaps at around a mile and a quarter*

Snaffles (Ire) 104p

3 b.c. Churchill (Ire) – Annabelle Ja (Fr) (Singspiel (Ire))
2021 7d^5 7g* p7g* Oct 1

Demi O'Byrne, for so long a key part of Coolmore's buying team, is no stranger to operating at the top-end of global bloodstock markets. Indeed, O'Byrne, representing Coolmore, made the winning $16-million bid for The Green Monkey, a record paid for a horse at auction. The Green Monkey was a notorious flop, failing to win from three starts, but O'Byrne did have plenty of notable success stories during a period when Coolmore established itself as the dominant player in the bloodstock world, with the likes of Camelot, High Chaparral and St Nicholas Abbey featuring among a plethora of purchases who proved to be money well spent.

O'Byrne, now operating with business partner Sean Grassick, offered a recent reminder that he can spot a bargain at a lower level when picking up Snaffles for just €11,000 at the 2020 Goffs Autumn Online Yearling Sale. Snaffles quickly showed that to be a shrewd purchase, winning two of his three starts as a juvenile in O'Byrne's red silks, including a listed race at Dundalk. Snaffles was too green to do himself justice when fifth on his debut at Leopardstown in August, but he duly improved for that experience and took a big step forward at Down Royal the following month, drawing five lengths clear in the style of one destined for much better things. That earned Snaffles a shot at a strong-looking edition of the listed Star Appeal Stakes at Dundalk in October and he proved well up to the task, quickening nicely to lead a furlong out and just needing to be driven out from there to win by three quarters of a length.

Snaffles was picked up cheaply, but he possesses an excellent pedigree, being a half-brother to three black-type performers, most notably Libranno, who registered a trio of Group 2 victories at up to seven furlongs. Al Muthana and Unforgetable were also best at around that trip, so there is plenty of pace in the pedigree. Snaffles himself has raced only at seven furlongs and the style of his victory at Dundalk suggests he is not in need of any further—speed rather than stamina was tested in that steadily-run event. ***Joseph O'Brien***

Conclusion: *Bargain buy who remains with potential after winning his final two starts of 2021, including a listed race at Dundalk*

Star of India (Ire) 91p

3 b.c. Galileo (Ire) – Shermeen (Ire) (Desert Style (Ire))
2021 7g* Oct 23

We're assuming that Star of India is named after one of the world's largest sapphires, kept at New York's American Museum of Natural History, and not the world's oldest operational sailing ship which bears the same name. But, who knows, maybe the inspiration is actually Michael Tabor's curry house of choice when he fancies a chicken tikka masala. There have been plenty of other Star of Indias before the current one who races in the Tabor colours for the Coolmore partners, notably the filly who was the champion two-year-old of 1955 in England when winning all five of her starts that year, all over five furlongs, earning an exceptional Timeform rating for a juvenile of 138.

The latest Star of India, a colt, was also unbeaten as a two-year-old, albeit from just the one start which he won in cosy fashion at Leopardstown in October. Joseph O'Brien saddled the even-money favourite in that 12-runner maiden, Sir Antonino, who had finished second on his debut in a similar event at the Curragh, but he had to settle for the runner-up spot again once Star of India led inside the final furlong. Having chased the leaders under Seamie Heffernan for most of the way, Star of India was pushed out to beat the favourite by two and a quarter lengths and he looks sure to progress from what was a very promising debut.

Entries for Ireland's classics close far earlier than their British counterparts and it's interesting that Star of India has been given an entry for the Irish Derby but not the Irish 2000 Guineas. That suggests connections are expecting him to take more after his sire Galileo than the dam's side of his pedigree which is predominantly all about speed. His dam, Shermeen, won three times over sprint trips at two and finished third in the Cornwallis Stakes on her final start in Britain, though she later won over eight and a half furlongs in the States. Shermeen's best foal was the smart Irish two-year-old sprinter Sudirman (by Henrythenavigator), who won the Railway Stakes and Phoenix Stakes over six furlongs. More of an indication of the way Star of India's three-year-old season might develop distance-wise comes from his year-older full brother Roman Empire, who had smart form over a mile and a quarter. He ended his two-year-old season by winning a maiden at Gowran over a mile and then finished fourth when given a pacemaking role in the Dante last year. He also ran well to finish second in the Hampton Court Stakes at Royal Ascot before being exported to Hong Kong. ***Aidan O'Brien***

Conclusion: *Promising winner of his only start in a late-season maiden and no surprise if he turns out at least as good as some smart siblings*

Tenebrism (USA) 115p

3 b.or br.f. Caravaggio (USA) – Immortal Verse (Ire) (Pivotal)

2021 5v* 6m* Sep 25

Missing a six-month chunk of the season would have written off many a two-year-old's campaign, but Tenebrism shrugged off her lengthy absence since the spring to prove herself the best filly of her generation in the autumn. She was Aidan O'Brien's first two-year-old runner of the year when beating eight other newcomers in heavy ground

Tenebrism produced a remarkable performance to win the Cheveley Park

at Naas at the end of March, quickening from last to first in the final two furlongs and pulling almost four lengths clear by the line. The same race had been won 12 months earlier, incidentally, by the future 2000 Guineas winner Poetic Flare. That ought to have booked Tenebrism's ticket to Royal Ascot, but she ended up missing not only the Royal meeting but all the other top summer races for two-year-old fillies.

Conditions were much firmer at Newmarket in September when Tenebrism finally returned to action in the Cheveley Park Stakes, a tall order for any filly with just one run under her belt (Regal Rose in 2000 had been the last to win it with such little experience), let alone one also returning from such a long absence. Even her own trainer had to admit 'I had a knot in my stomach whether it was fair to be running her or not.' But O'Brien needn't have worried. After a slow start, Tenebrism again had to come from well off the pace but, once Ryan Moore shook her up from halfway, she picked up really well against the stand rail to lead in the final 50 yards. Flotus was a length behind her in second, with a three-length break to the Albany and Duchess of Cambridge Stakes winner Sandrine in third. The way we read the form, that was a better effort than the one Inspiral put up to keep her own unbeaten record in the Fillies' Mile the following month.

Tenebrism was a first winner for her sire, the high-class sprinter Caravaggio, and her Cheveley Park victory went a long way towards making him the leading first-season sire. The way Tenebrism finished at Newmarket suggests she'll stay at least another furlong and the racing record of her dam offers further encouragement that she'll stay the Guineas trip. French filly Immortal Verse finished down the field in her own country's version of the 1000 Guineas, but she improved considerably to win the Coronation Stakes at Royal Ascot with a sharp turn of foot—something her daughter has clearly inherited—and took the scalp of star miler Goldikova in the Prix Jacques le Marois with a similar burst of speed. If the sturdy Tenebrism proves just as effective at a mile herself, she'll have every chance of becoming her stable's sixth 1000 Guineas winner in seven years. ***Aidan O'Brien***

Conclusion: *Overcame lengthy absence to stamp herself the best of her sex at two in the Cheveley Park on just her second start and looks a leading 1000 Guineas contender*

SECTION 3

TALKING TO THE TRAINERS

To give some pointers for the new season, we asked a number of leading Flat trainers to pick out a star performer, handicapper and dark horse to follow from their respective stables. Read on to find out which names came back...

Michael Bell

Wins-Runs in Britain in 2021	**50-325**
Highest-rated horse in training	**Zeeband** Timeform Rating 104

Star Performer: Dillian (103): "He won his maiden very nicely but was too green and raw to do himself justice in the Group 1 in France. His pedigree suggests he will improve with time and distance."

Handicapper: Shivraj (58p): "He is obviously bred in the purple and I think the handicapper has given him a chance off 62. There should be room to manoeuvre."

Dark Horse: Present Moment (83p): "She won her maiden nicely. She is a May foal, so hopefully she could work her way up the ladder."

Marco Botti

Wins-Runs in Britain in 2021	**50-399**
Highest-rated horse in training	**Felix** Timeform Rating 112

Star Performer: Ribbon Rose (80p): "I was really impressed with the way she won her maiden at Newmarket last year. She was a tall, leggy, two-year-old but has come back from her winter break looking a lot stronger. She has a bit of something about her."

Handicapper: Silver Gunn (89): "He won three times last year finishing up on a rating of 81. He was gelded over the winter break and I hope it will bring about some improvement. He looks a nice middle-distance/staying prospect with age and maturity."

Dark Horse: Sousa (unraced): "An unraced three-year-old who came from the breeze-up sales in 2021. He is by Exceed and Excel, who I've had success with before with horses such as Excelebration. He went a little weak last year, but we've given him some time off to strengthen and I'm delighted with how he has come back. He looks a nice prospect for 2022."

George Boughey

Wins-Runs in Britain in 2021	**84-465**
Highest-rated horse in training	**Cachet** Timeform Rating 104

Star Performer: Cachet (104): "She will be programmed on the traditional English classic route. Some of her best performances have been on the Rowley Mile and she is likely to start in the Nell Gwyn. She is the highest-rated horse in our yard at the moment but yet to win a stakes race. She seems to have done as well as I had hoped over the winter and is back cantering."

Handicapper: Pocket The Profit (88): "He was a prolific winner at the backend of 2021 and I hope he will be able to resume his progress when stepped back up in trip. He is not a big horse but one with a great will to win and I would hope he can take a step forward again. Being by Mayson and having already shown a liking for soft ground, we may plot him carefully on slower ground."

Dark Horse: Phantasy Mac (57p): "She showed up well in novices at two but was a touch on the weak side and couldn't finish her races out. I hope she will improve at three—her pedigree and physique suggest that she might."

Owen Burrows

Wins-Runs in Britain in 2021	**22-126**
Highest-rated horse in training	**Hukum** Timeform Rating 124

Star Performer: Minzaal (117): "He obviously missed most of last season but showed he retains plenty of ability by finishing third in the Champions Sprint on only his second start of the year. I thought that was a massive run considering he'd only made his debut two weeks earlier. Hopefully, we can have a clear run with him this year and all the big sprints will be on his agenda. He'll probably start at York in May and I'm really looking forward to him."

Handicapper: Washraa (84): "A lovely scopey filly who had three runs last year, finishing second the last twice. I think she was unfortunate to bump into a couple of nice horses, so a mark of 78 looks workable. She's done well physically over the winter and should get a mile in time."

Dark Horse: Unnamed two-year-old colt out of Myturn (unraced): "With Shadwell reducing their numbers I don't really have any dark horses unfortunately. I have some

Owen Burrows poses with his smart sprinter Minzaal

lovely two-year-olds, all unnamed at the moment, though. A few to look out for from mid-season are a Churchill/Myturn colt, a Siyouni/Anasheed colt and a Dubawi/ Alaflaak filly."

Henry Candy

Wins-Runs in Britain in 2021	**18-170**
Highest-rated horse in training	**Run To Freedom** Timeform Rating 107

Star Performer: By Starlight (93): "She has always been a very tall filly and is now hopefully strengthening up. Hopefully, she will be capable of earning some black type this year."

Handicapper: Maiden Castle (97): "He is still reasonably handicapped and should win a race or two this year. He is not the soundest but seems to be okay at the moment."

Dark Horse: Sainte Colette (unraced): "She is a typical Mastercraftsman filly who will take time to mature. She is from a good family and will hopefully be nice as the year progresses."

Mick Channon

Wins-Runs in Britain in 2021	**46-551**
Highest-rated horse in training	**Chairmanoftheboard** Timeform Rating 102

Star Performer: Kinrarra (70): "She ran twice for us last year. She has matured and developed over the winter and I'm excited to see her back on the racecourse this year. She is a cracking filly and a great middle-distance prospect."

Handicapper: Wonderful World (90): "He had a slight setback around the middle of last year but won a handicap at the backend of the season. I'm looking forward to see him back this year as a three-year-old."

Dark Horse: Baroque Star (75): "She is another cracking filly who will love middle-distances."

Michael Dods

Wins-Runs in Britain in 2021	**56-503**
Highest-rated horse in training	**Commanche Falls** Timeform Rating 114

Star Performer: Blackrod (104): "A four-year-old colt who had a tremendous season in 2021. He is rated 95 and I could see him getting black type this season, an improving horse still definitely on the upgrade."

Handicapper: Azure Blue (77): "She is an interesting filly and well rated off 78. I would expect her to do well in 2022. She has grown and strengthened up over the winter. Six or seven furlongs will probably be her trip."

Dark Horse: Chiellini (unraced): "He could be a horse to watch in 2022. An unraced three-year-old, he is by Aclaim and a half-brother to Que Amoro. He looks the type to do well and will improve with time."

Ed Dunlop

Wins-Runs in Britain in 2021	**29-318**
Highest-rated horse in training	**Red Verdon** Timeform Rating 112

Star Performer: John Leeper (111): "He showed a lot of promise early on in his three-year-old season. He won his first two starts, including the listed Fairway Stakes at Newmarket, before heading off to the Derby. His form dipped a bit towards the backend of last season, but he has since enjoyed a healthy break. He looks in good order and we will look to target some long-distance stakes races for him this season."

Handicapper: Haunted Dream (82p): "He has already made an impression whilst competing in handicaps. On only his second handicap start as a two-year-old, he galloped to a clear four-length victory at Chelmsford over a mile and a quarter. His pedigree and attitude would suggest he is the type of horse who will improve into his three-year-old campaign and I am hopeful he will be running in some nice handicaps this season."

Dark Horse: Wendell's Lad (77p): "He is a three-year-old son of New Approach who has been shining brightly at home. He made an impressive late run when finishing third on his debut earlier this year. He is a big scopey individual who promises to progress. We will aim him towards novices and step him up gradually from there."

Charlie Fellowes

Wins-Runs in Britain in 2021	**38-316**
Highest-rated horse in training	**Vadream** Timeform Rating 114

Star Performer: Vadream (114): "She developed into a top-class sprinter at the end of last year, winning the Bengough Stakes and looking a shade unlucky in the Champions Sprint. There is no reason why she can't go close at the top level, especially on soft ground which she clearly loves."

Handicapper: Injazati (106): "He progressed very nicely last year before appearing to not quite get home at Newmarket in the Old Rowley Cup. He is a lovely big horse who should be even better this year."

Dark Horse: Purple Ribbon (99p): "She has won two of her three starts so far. She is officially rated 90 now and from a family that improve with age, so we would like to think that she can improve into a pattern performer this year."

William Haggas

Wins-Runs in Britain in 2021	**174-700**
Highest-rated horse in training	**Baaeed** Timeform Rating 130

Star Performer: Sacred (115): "She is a very talented filly who loves fast ground. I think she runs best when fresh and that was probably the biggest contributing factor in her defeat in the 1000 Guineas. She relaxes well enough to get a mile and, if she does, options will be plentiful."

Sacred quickened well to win the Hungerford Stakes

Handicapper: Pride of Priory (94p): "He only won a two-horse race at Haydock but impressed me. He did not run again but has done well and should have a fruitful campaign as he steps up in trip."

Dark Horse: Sea Tsarina (unraced): "She is a full sister to Sea Empress, a hugely talented filly who ultimately proved disappointing. This filly is stronger, will be faster and has a good attitude and way of going."

Charlie Hills

Wins-Runs in Britain in 2021	**75-474**
Highest-rated horse in training	**Equilateral/Pogo** Timeform Rating 118

Star Performer: Equilateral (118): "He is cantering away and remains one of the fastest horses I have trained. He will target the big sprints this summer."

Handicapper: Dark Shift (101): "He will be aimed at some valuable handicaps this year. He is versatile having won over trips ranging from six furlongs to a mile."

Dark Horse: Wanees (82p): "He is one of our smartest three-year-olds this year. He won twice last year over seven furlongs and is bred to stay further. I hope he will make up into a Group 1 horse this season."

David Menuisier

Wins-Runs in Britain in 2021 **21-188**

Highest-rated horse in training **Migration** Timeform Rating 115

Star Performer: Migration (115): "He had a great season in 2021 following 18 months on the sidelines. He is highly rated and can hopefully make an impact in black-type races in 2022."

Handicapper: Flyin' Solo (98): "He showed good potential last year and should benefit from a gelding operation before this season. He is stoutly bred on the dam's side of his pedigree and he will hopefully keep on improving as his stamina is tested."

Dark Horse: Findono (85p): "He only ran once last year at three, finishing third in a good maiden at Newbury last spring. He was subsequently sidelined through injury and was given time to mature physically. He should be one to keep on the right side of when he is fully tuned up."

Kevin Ryan

Wins-Runs in Britain in 2021 **79-612**

Highest-rated horse in training **Emaraaty Ana** Timeform Rating 120

Star Performer: Emaraaty Ana (120): "He was placed in the Nunthorpe and went on to win the Sprint Cup before a fine effort in the Breeders' Cup Turf Sprint. He is a horse we always thought was capable of winning at the highest level and it's great to see him fulfilling that. He is likely to head to Dubai for the Al Quoz Sprint and then he will run in the top Group 1 sprints here this season."

Handicapper: Dark Moon Rising (92): "He improved with each run last year and enjoyed stepping up in trip. It was great to see him winning as he was certainly not the finished article and he is a horse who should progress with age. He starts on a mark of 90 and could be a nice three-year-old for races over a mile and a quarter through the year."

Dark Horse: The Cookstown Cafu (81): "He improved with each run and was unlucky to just get headed on his final start. We know the family well and they have progressed with time, so hopefully he can go on from his two-year-old season. He is still a maiden but starts with a fair mark of 79 and was another who looked more likely to make up into a three-year-old."

Happy connections after Emaraaty Ana's victory in the Sprint Cup

James Tate

Wins-Runs in Britain in 2021	**31-223**
Highest-rated horse in training	**Garden Paradise** Timeform Rating 109

Star Performer: Garden Paradise (109): "This big, rangy Night of Thunder filly improved dramatically last year to win a listed race over a mile and a half at Kempton in November. She should progress again this year and is likely to be targeted at fillies' races like the Lillie Langtry at Goodwood and Park Hill at Doncaster."

Handicapper: Ocean Wave (89): "She is a tall, rangy Le Havre filly who won her last two starts in 2021 and is expected to improve again this year. She will start off in handicaps, but I'm hoping she will progress into a black-type filly."

Dark Horse: Royal Aclaim (86p): "She is a big, strong Aclaim filly who won her only start as a two-year-old, beating a subsequent Group 1 winner [Perfect Power] and a subsequent listed winner [Fearby]. She is a very fast filly."

Roger Varian

Wins-Runs in Britain in 2021	**131-615**
Highest-rated horse in training	**Eshaada** Timeform Rating 120p

Star Performer: Teona (120): "She progressed wonderfully last season, starting the campaign with only a Newcastle maiden win under her belt and finishing it as a Group 1 winner courtesy of her victory in the Prix Vermeille at Longchamp. She then ran an excellent race when third in the Breeders' Cup Turf and I'm looking forward to another exciting season with her."

Handicapper: Legend of Dubai (87): "A lightly raced four-year-old, he was second to subsequent Irish Derby runner-up Lone Eagle on his final start at two and then won his only outing last season at Ffos Las. He begins handicapping off a mark of 85 and I would be hopeful he can prove better than that."

Dark Horse: Zanbaq (86p): "A winner on her only start as a two-year-old at Kempton last November, she has done well over the winter and I am excited to see what she can develop into as a three-year-old."

Ed Walker

Wins-Runs in Britain in 2021	**65-409**
Highest-rated horse in training	**Came From The Dark** Timeform Rating 119

Star Performer: Great Ambassador (114p): "He did nothing but improve last year and, with a bit more luck, he could have won at least one major sprint handicap. He proved he is more than up to stakes class when winning the Garrowby and I think he could be competitive at the highest level this year. He will hopefully start in the Duke of York."

Handicapper: Parachute (99): "He went so close at Royal Ascot before having a disappointing second half of the season. He is better than that and has now been gelded. He could progress to be a top-end staying handicapper this year."

Dark Horse: Bling On The Music (74p): "He is a colt I have loved since day one. He disappointed on debut but was very big and raw last year. He has done very well and I hope he can make into a smart performer."

RISING STARS

Alice Haynes

Base	**Newmarket, Suffolk**
First full licence	**2021**
First winner	**Act of Magic** Wolverhampton 12/03/2021
Total winners	**24**
Best Flat horse trained	**Mr Professor** Timeform Rating 99

Alice Haynes' first season with a licence in 2021 comfortably exceeded the goals she'd set herself at the start of the year. Starting out with a string of around 15 horses, a target of 10 winners was the aim in her first season. The Newmarket yard sent out its first runners at the end of February and already had a couple of winners on the board by the time the turf season started. Winner number 10 came when two-year-old filly Hollow Steel won for the second time, in a nursery at Thirsk at the beginning of August, and by the end of the year, that tally had been doubled. Josies Kid, who won a nursery at York, and Gin O'Clock, who won a novice at Chelmsford on the second of his two starts and looks potentially useful, were two of the yard's better two-year-olds, but it was the arrival of Mr Professor during the summer which did most to raise his trainer's profile. He'd shown just modest form in three starts for Joseph Tuite but showed considerable improvement on his first appearance for Haynes when stepped up to a mile for his nursery debut at Kempton in September. Mr Professor followed up in good style in a similar event at Bath a week later and ended his two-year-old campaign by taking his form up another level, springing a 16/1 surprise in the listed Silver Tankard Stakes at Pontefract. Mr Professor has since run well at the Dubai Carnival and his success in the colours of Kia Joorabchian's Amo Racing obviously has the potential to encourage further support from one of racing's biggest new owners. Another to advertise his trainer's skills was sprinter Strong Power, who rattled off a quick hat-trick over five furlongs at Lingfield in Haynes' own colours in January, breaking the track record for the second of those wins. From an equestrian background, including competing in eventing, Haynes' involvement in racing began as a 16-year-old with Henrietta Knight's yard before later joining Mick Channon and then David Simcock. It was for Simcock that she rode the majority of her nine winners on the Flat, though her tenth and final success in the saddle came as an amateur over hurdles at Stratford in 2019. Before making the decision to take out a licence of her own, Haynes did pre-training of young horses for the likes of Roger Varian and William Haggas.

Grant Tuer

Base	**Birkby, North Yorkshire**
First full licence	**2006**
First winner	**Backsheesh** Market Rasen 16/03/2002
Total winners	**122**
Best Flat horse trained	**Illusionist/Lion Tower** Timeform Rating 96

Not many stables are able to maintain a 20% strike rate over the course of a Flat season. Those that equalled or bettered that mark in 2021 included champion trainer Charlie Appleby, along with fellow Newmarket trainers William Haggas, Sir Michael Stoute, Saeed bin Suroor, Roger Varian and John & Thady Gosden, all of them, of course, well established among the country's most successful yards. Much further down the prize-money table—outside the top 60, in fact—was North Yorkshire trainer Grant Tuer, but that only made his achievement of also hitting a one in five success rate all the more praiseworthy. The stable's top earner was four-year-old gelding Lion Tower whose most valuable success came in a 0-85 handicap at Musselburgh. As one who managed to keep a step ahead of the handicapper, Lion Tower was typical of the sort of horse that Tuer's highly successful season was built upon. Lion Tower won four of his eight starts, sprinter Gunnerside, in the trainer's own colours, won six out of 10, and Out of Breath completed a five-timer in June and July. With a Timeform rating of 96, Lion Tower and Illusionist, who won sprint handicaps at Hamilton and York, are tied at the top among the best horses Tuer has trained so far. The names listed above were the main contributors to a much-improved seasonal total in 2021 which easily surpassed the stable's previous best annual score of 21 set in 2019. When Blazing Hot won at Wolverhampton a week before Christmas, as well as being the stable's forty-ninth and final success of the year, he also brought up a career total of 100 winners on the Flat for his trainer. Tuer's earliest successes had come when riding—as well as training—his own pointers, the most successful of which was Son of Anshan, who won four hunter chases for Tuer and finished third in the Fox Hunters' at Aintree in 2002. However, the current chapter of Tuer's career, when returning from farming full-time to resume training again, began in 2016 when, on the retirement of his father Edwin, he took over the licence of the family's Wiske House Farm Stables at Birkby not far from Catterick. An increased string, along with investment in the yard's facilities, including an improved gallop, and some shrewd placing of his runners were behind Tuer's eye-catching results in 2021 and further progress looks assured. One final thing to note—unlike those bigger yards with the best strike rates, backing Tuer's runners blind in 2021 would have resulted in a level-stakes profit.

Hector Crouch

Attached stable	**Ralph Beckett**
First ride	**2013**
First winner	**Whinging Willie** Newbury 24/6/2014
Total winners in Britain	**308**
Best horse ridden	**Desert Fire** Timeform Rating 118

Barring the Covid-hit season of 2020, Hector Crouch's number of winners has steadily increased each year since riding his first winners in 2014, and when Morani Kali won at Kempton in November, it took his year's total to a new seasonal best of 64 wins. Another pleasing aspect to Crouch's stats in 2021 was his 16% strike rate, a marked improvement on previous seasons and indicative of him picking up better rides. A graduate from pony racing, Crouch started out as an apprentice for Gary Moore and rode his first winner for the yard in June 2014 when Whinging Willie was successful in an apprentice race at Newbury. Moore supplied the majority of Crouch's early winners and remains one of his main supporters, though Saeed bin Suroor was among the other trainers to start using Crouch's services as a 7 lb claimer. In the winter of 2015/16, Crouch widened his horizons by riding in Dubai, mainly for UAE champion trainer Sateesh Seemar, something the jockey described as 'a massive learning curve'. Back in Britain, Crouch rode his first winners for Ralph Beckett in 2016 and for Clive Cox in 2017, two more yards which have been instrumental in Crouch's success ever since, particularly in the latest season when they accounted for the majority of his winners between them. A four-timer at Lingfield in July 2017 was an early highlight during Crouch's apprentice days and on Boxing Day of the same year he had his first win in the Godolphin colours on Ocean of Love at Wolverhampton before riding out his claim shortly afterwards. It was Cox who provided Crouch's first group winner when Streamline won the Sirenia Stakes at Kempton in September 2019, while Crouch's first ride in a classic came for Bin Suroor on Military March, who finished fourth in the 2000 Guineas in 2020. More rides for Beckett in 2021 resulted in Crouch riding his first Royal Ascot winner when Surefire won the King George V Stakes, and a partnership with the same stable's smart Victory Chimes yielded three wins, including a listed contest at Goodwood. Crouch returned to Dubai to ride at the Carnival for Bin Suroor early this year and was rewarded with a Group 2 victory on the stable's second string Desert Fire in the Al Rashidiya.

Harry Davies

Attached stable	**Andrew Balding**
First ride	**2022**
First winner	**Coolagh Magic** Lingfield 14/1/2022
Total winners in Britain	**5**
Best horse(s) ridden	**Power of States** Timeform Rating 105

Riding a first winner in the Godolphin colours must be a memorable moment for any young jockey, but it was probably all the more so for Harry Davies. Not only was Tranquil Night the 17-year-old's first ride for Godolphin and Charlie Appleby, but his win in the Kempton novice in February, with his 7 lb claim effectively negating the horse's penalty, came less than a month after his very first ride under Rules at Southwell. But the fact that Tranquil Night was already the jockey's fourth winner shows what a flying start he has made to his professional career this year. In fact, Davies' first winner, Coolagh Magic, whom he produced to lead on the line for a nose win in an apprentice handicap at Lingfield for Robyn Brisland, came on just his second ride. He then made it two out of three on Desert Lime for George Boughey at Wolverhampton three days later. Davies was champion on the pony racing circuit in 2018 and 2019 and from the age of just seven had ambitions to eventually join Andrew Balding's yard in the hope of following in the footsteps of the likes of David Probert, William Buick and Oisin Murphy, who all learned their craft as apprentices at Kingsclere. On the eve of his win for Godolphin, Davies rode his first winner for Balding when Hold Fast won an apprentice handicap at Kempton. He also has close connections with Hugo Palmer's Newmarket yard where his mother Angie is assistant trainer, while Boughey has supplied him with plenty of his early mounts. Davies is well placed to pick up rides as his agent is his stepfather Phil Shea, who has had the likes of recent champion apprentices Josephine Gordon and Cieren Fallon on his books. Like Fallon, Davies is following his father into the profession as Stephen Davies was himself champion apprentice in 1994, riding 45 winners that season when attached to Henry Cecil's yard.

CLASSIC ANTE-POST

Timeform's Feature Writer John Ingles takes a look at the markets for the first four classics and picks out his value bets . . .

It's Platinum Jubilee year and events to mark the Queen's 70 years on the throne include the creation of a four-day bank holiday weekend at the beginning of June which, of course, also happens to coincide with both Oaks and Derby Day. 45 years ago, Her Majesty enjoyed one of her most successful years as an owner thanks to her filly Dunfermline who won the Oaks and St Leger in 1977, the year of her Silver Jubilee. There hasn't been a royal Derby winner during the Queen's reign, though just four days after her Coronation in 1953, her top-class colt Aureole finished runner-up at Epsom. Some bookmakers are offering single-figure odds about the Queen's Reach For The Moon getting into the spirit of Jubilee weekend and going one better on June 4. The classic prospects of him and many others are discussed below in the hope of unearthing another Mother Earth, recommended each-way at 25/1 for the 1000 Guineas here last year. That too would be something to celebrate!

2000 Guineas

Charlie Appleby has enjoyed worldwide success, including three winners at last year's Breeders' Cup alone, but he has yet to win either of the two Guineas on his own doorstep. There's a good chance that he'll put that right in 2022 with Godolphin looking to hold a strong hand in the first colts' classic. One of those Breeders' Cup winners, **Modern Games**, confirmed his smart effort in the Tattersalls Stakes at Newmarket by winning the Juvenile Turf at Del Mar in good style on his first try at a mile. But stronger claims are held by stablemates **Native Trail** and **Coroebus**. Group 1 wins in the National Stakes and Dewhurst Stakes established Native Trail as last year's top two-year-old and physically he's very much the type to progress further at three. But on the same card as the Dewhurst there was plenty to like about the way Coroebus, another really taking sort on looks, travelled through the race and settled matters in the Autumn Stakes over the Rowley Mile. Coroebus made his debut a couple of months later than Native Trail and had one race less last year, so it could well be that he has the more progress to make at three. As such, he looks the one to give his trainer a first Newmarket classic.

Aidan O'Brien already has plenty of those, of course, though his pair of colts prominent in the 2000 Guineas betting may well need further than a mile this year. **Point Lonsdale**, a brother to his stable's very smart mile and a half performer Broome, met

Coroebus (royal blue) looks a major contender for the 2000 Guineas

with his first defeat when coming up against Native Trail in the National Stakes, whereas **Luxembourg** remained unbeaten when signing off with a win in heavy ground in the Vertem Futurity Trophy. His stable's last couple of 2000 Guineas winners won the same race at Doncaster, as did his sire Camelot, but Epsom rather than Newmarket might provide his better chance of following in his father's classic footsteps.

For **Perfect Power**, on the other hand, the mile could prove too much of a stretch. He enjoyed a fine two-year-old season as a sprinter, though the Middle Park Stakes he won on his final start was a messy race. Solario Stakes winner **Reach For The Moon** will have to have recovered from injury to be a Guineas contender and his narrow odds-on defeat to subsequent Dewhurst and Futurity Trophy third **Bayside Boy** in the Champagne Stakes at Doncaster leaves him with a bit to find. Vintage Stakes winner **Angel Bleu** found further improvement to complete a Group 1 double in France in the autumn, though how much more improvement there is to come from him remains to be seen.

Of those at longer odds who could further their claims with a good trial in the spring are **Light Infantry**, who made it two out of two in the Horris Hill Stakes at Newbury, and the Ballydoyle colt **Star of India**, who made quite a taking debut in a maiden at Leopardstown.

Recommendation: Coroebus (5/1)

1000 Guineas

The 1000 Guineas has a clear favourite in **Inspiral** following an unbeaten four-race campaign for John and Thady Gosden at two. The daughter of Frankel certainly made a good impression, impressing in a listed race at Sandown, running out a clear-cut winner of the May Hill Stakes at Doncaster and then dominant again when winning the Fillies' Mile after travelling strongly into contention. That's already better form than her dam Starscope showed when finishing runner-up at 33/1 in the Guineas and, so far at least, Inspiral has shown no sign of the unsatisfactory temperament which landed her dam with a Timeform 'squiggle'. But convincing though Inspiral was, there wasn't much strength in depth to the Fillies' Mile in which she was chased home by Prosperous Voyage, also runner-up in the May Hill, who isn't even quoted in most lists for the 1000 Guineas.

The last three 1000 Guineas winners had all been placed in the Fillies' Mile, but it's hard to see that trend being maintained. All three of those were trained by Aidan O'Brien whose other 1000 Guineas winners include Minding, who was the last filly to complete the Fillies' Mile/Guineas double in 2016. Ballydoyle's main Guineas hope this year comes from the Cheveley Park Stakes instead and, judged strictly on form, there's an argument for its winner **Tenebrism** to be ahead of Inspiral in the Guineas

Inspiral heads the ante-post betting for the 1000 Guineas

betting. Yes, she's by sprinter Caravaggio and is yet to race beyond six furlongs herself, prompting stamina concerns, but her dam is the high-class French miler Immortal Verse and Tenebrism, in rear for most of the way, saw the Cheveley Park out really strongly when leading only in the last 50 yards. That was some achievement given it was only her second start and came after a six-month absence following an impressive winning debut in the spring. That lack of experience might encourage her trainer to give her another run before the Guineas and would also tell us more about her potential to see out the mile. At more than twice the price of Inspiral in most lists, Tenebrism is a tempting alternative to the favourite.

However, the one who makes most appeal is another filly who ended the year with a Group 1 win, **Discoveries**. That came in the Moyglare Stud Stakes at the Curragh where she knuckled down well to turn the tables on the pair who finished in front of her in the Debutante Stakes, **Agartha** and **Sunset Shiraz**, while back in fourth was the Ballydoyle filly **Concert Hall**, who was beaten a similar distance behind Inspiral at Newmarket. If Discoveries improves further from two to three in the same way her high-class siblings Alpha Centauri and Alpine Star did for Jessica Harrington when stepping up to a mile, odds of 16/1 in places for the 1000 Guineas are going to look very generous.

Recommendation: Discoveries (16/1)

The Derby

Some of the colts who feature prominently in the 2000 Guineas market head the Derby betting, and while there are good reasons on pedigree for thinking **Luxembourg** and **Point Lonsdale** will stay the trip, as touched on above, **Native Trail**, a son of sprinter Oasis Dream, makes far less appeal than either of those at single-figure odds for Epsom. Luxembourg is a worthy winter favourite, though no doubt the spring trials will reveal other leading contenders currently at much longer prices and it's some of those types we'll try to uncover here.

First, though, another of those prominent in the betting already mentioned in the 2000 Guineas preview is **Reach For The Moon**, potentially the Queen's best chance of owning a Derby winner for the first time since Carlton House finished a close third as the 5/2 favourite in 2011. By a Derby winner in Sea The Stars, Reach For The Moon's brother Chalk Stream is a smart winner at a mile and a half and his dam is a sister to Her Majesty's Oaks runner-up Flight of Fancy, so he's certainly no forlorn hope to stay the trip on pedigree.

John and Thady Gosden have another Sea The Stars colt among the top half-dozen or so in the betting with **Antarah**, who landed the odds on his debut at Newcastle in October, earning Timeform's large 'P' symbol reserved for especially promising types.

Reach For The Moon (centre) would be a popular winner for his owner

The same stable's **Magisterial** figures in the *Fifty* after his decisive win second time out at Haydock the same month. He's by Frankel, sire of last year's Derby winner Adayar, and is a half-brother to Coronation Stakes winner Lillie Langtry whose daughter Tuesday is mentioned below as an Oaks contender.

Nottingham maidens are worth keeping an eye on late in the season, and a couple of impressive winning debutants from such races to find their way into our *Fifty* are **Desert Crown** and **Eldar Eldarov**, trained by Sir Michael Stoute and Roger Varian respectively. Both earned large 'P' symbols for their clear-cut victories, expensive breeze-up purchase Eldar Eldarov being all the rage for his debut whereas Desert Crown's win in the Derby-winning 'Kris Kin' colours of Mr Saeed Suhail was evidently more unexpected but no less impressive.

At a higher level, a race which could easily throw up some Derby types is the Criterium de Saint-Cloud which was dominated by British and Irish stables. The James Ferguson-trained winner **El Bodegon** benefitted from an enterprising ride, but runner-up **Stone Age** and fourth-placed **Buckaroo**—for Aidan and Joseph O'Brien respectively— shaped well behind him. Galileo's son Stone Age is still a maiden, but he was campaigned at two like a top horse (touched off in a Group 2 at Leopardstown on Irish Champions' Weekend) and can only improve further over a mile and a half, while Buckaroo, who beat Stone Age in a maiden at Galway, is crying out for longer trips, too.

Recommendations: Desert Crown (40/1 e/w), Stone Age (50/1 e/w)

The Oaks

Inspiral also heads the betting in an otherwise shapeless ante-post market for the Oaks. Between them, John Gosden and Aidan O'Brien have won the last eight editions of the Oaks. Gosden's most recent winner, Anapurna, was also a daughter of Frankel, so Inspiral isn't totally without merit as a potential winner, but you get the feeling she's just a placeholder at the head of the betting over the winter until stronger contenders and later developers emerge in the trials. Not that the Oaks winner is always a totally unexposed filly who just had the one run at two, such as Enable. O'Brien's last two Oaks winners, Love and Snowfall, were very much hiding in plain sight as two-year-olds, both running seven times and being beaten in the Fillies' Mile (in which Snowfall finished eighth of ten at 50/1!). **Concert Hall**, mentioned above, winner of the Weld Park Stakes between those defeats in the Moyglare and Fillies' Mile, has a similar profile to that pair and has the added recommendation of being out of an Oaks winner, Was.

The much less exposed Santa Barbara was Ballydoyle's main classic hope among its fillies last season and the once-raced **Tuesday** is in a similar mould this year. She shaped very well when beaten a short head by none other than Discoveries in a maiden at the Curragh last June but, unlike the winner, wasn't seen out again. Her Oaks odds could tumble if she goes one better in a similar event on her return in the spring and, as a sister to Oaks winner Minding, she's another with just the right sort of pedigree. Stable-companion **History**, a daughter of Galileo who cost 2.8m guineas as a yearling, got off the mark on her third attempt at two in a maiden at Gowran and is another who could easily strengthen her Oaks claims in the spring.

For an each-way recommendation, though, we'll go for Inspiral's stable-companion **Natasha**, she too a daughter of Frankel. It seemed significant that the Gosdens were prepared to throw her in the deep end when she contested the Prix Marcel Boussac in October and she clearly didn't give her true running at Longchamp, when there was almost certainly more to her disappointing display than the soft ground. She finished last in the end after being the first off the bridle, but that contrasted with how well she'd travelled when winning novice events on her two previous starts at Kempton and Sandown. A half-sister to the top-class French colt Almanzor, Natasha looked an exciting middle-distance prospect after those two wins and, given that it looks safe to put a line through her run in France, she looks overpriced at 50/1 in places for Epsom..

Recommendations: Natasha (50/1 e/w)

TOP ON TIME

Timing expert Graeme North highlights seven horses who proved themselves on the clock and have interesting profiles for the coming season.

Cash (Ire)

3 gr.c. Shamardal (USA) – Lady Rosamunde (Maria's Mon (USA))

It ought to be less of a risk shelling out large sums of money for a two-year-old at the breeze-up sales than it is buying for the same price as a yearling, and the £140,000 paid for Cash already looks as if it might be decent value. Cash has had only one run so far, namely a maiden at Newmarket in October, but he won it in excellent style and in a very fast time to boot for the type of race, his 87 timefigure one of the best posted all season by a winning newcomer over seven furlongs. By Shamardal out of a mare who won over a mile and three quarters, Cash will prove well suited by at least a mile and a half as a three-year-old. *David Simcock*

Dark Moon Rising (Ire)

3 b.c. Night of Thunder (Ire) – Al Nassa (USA) (Bernardini (USA))

Dark Moon Rising showed improved form on his final outing as a two-year-old, when finishing third on his nursery debut at York, and he has all the makings of a useful performer at three. The winner of a Beverley maiden in June, Dark Moon Rising posted faster timefigures still on his next two starts, including a 90 when competing off a BHA mark of 89 on the Knavesmire. Those up with the pace that day emerged with more credit than those held up given the strong gallop and the winner Oh Herberts Reign, with whom Dark Moon Rising disputed the running, followed up off a 6 lb higher mark next time. Dark Moon Rising's dam stayed a mile and a half, and he'll almost certainly stay a mile and a quarter. *Kevin Ryan*

Dark Shift

4 gr.c. Dark Angel (Ire) – Mosuo (Ire) (Oasis Dream)

A member of our *Fifty*, Dark Shift's performances on the clock last season are just one more reason to recommend him. Four wins from eight starts is no mean record, but the progress Dark Shift made on his final two starts last term suggests the penny had finally dropped for the promising son of Dark Angel. Both those wins came at Ascot, suggesting other big handicaps like the Victoria Cup or Hunt Cup might be on the agenda further down the line, and a 98 timefigure stacks up well against his current BHA mark of 91. It's worth reiterating that he is very much one to bear in mind for the Lincoln, particularly as he won first-time-out in both 2020 and 2021. *Charlie Hills*

Dark Moon Rising and High Fibre met in a nursery at York in October

High Fibre (Ire)

3 b.c. Vadamos (Fr) – Multi Grain (Sir Percy)

High Fibre was something of a slow burner as a two-year-old, but he blew apart what looked a competitive nursery at Newmarket on his final start, winning by five lengths and posting a 90 timefigure, well in excess of the BHA mark of 75 he ran off. High Fibre had suggested a run like that was in the offing when running the fastest final furlong on his previous appearance—and first for nearly three months—in the York nursery contested by Dark Moon Rising. Out of a mare who stayed a mile and a half, High Fibre will relish that trip himself. *Ralph Beckett*

Jazz Club (Ire)

3 b.c. Starspangledbanner (Aus) – Princess Desire (Ire) (Danehill (USA))

One of the fastest timefigures recorded by a two-year-old last season relative to their form rating was by Jazz Club in the valuable sales event at Doncaster's St Leger Festival. By their very nature sales races tend to be a mixed bag, but the level at the front of this contest was higher than is often the case and, in cutting out the running in first-time blinkers and pulling over three lengths clear of the fourth, Jazz Club posted a 105 timefigure. That run followed a Windsor win also achieved in a fast time and, with further progress on the cards, he should be up to making an impact in pattern company as a three-year-old. *Roger Varian*

Ribhi (Ire)

3 gr.c. Dark Angel (Ire) – Rihaam (Ire) (Dansili)

Ribhi might have fluffed his lines the only time he has tackled listed company, but inexperience probably caught him out that day on just his second start and the manner of his wins either side suggest he's probably got a race at that level in him when things drop right. Indeed, Ribhi was one of only a handful of two-years-olds last season to record a timefigure of 89 or higher on debut when thundering home at Salisbury, and so long as his temperament can be kept in check—he bolted to post on his third intended start—this powerful, rangy sort ought to excel at up to a mile. *Marcus Tregoning*

War Horse (Ire)

3 b.g. Sea The Stars (Ire) – Santa Anabaa (Exceed And Excel (Aus))

Marco Botti has had a couple of relatively quiet years and, by his own admission, he hasn't been helped by having some of his better horses being sold on to race elsewhere. Botti looks to have a couple of decent young prospects for 2022, however, and War Horse might well be the best of them. Three runs as a two-year-old saw War Horse improve his times steadily and his Goodwood maiden win on his final start, in an 82 timefigure, was even more meritorious given he had to overcome trouble in-running. He can go handicapping off a BHA mark of 83 and this son of Sea The Stars should come into his own when stepping up in trip to a mile and a half. *Marco Botti.*

Marco Botti has a couple of good prospects to go to war with in 2022

FIRST-SEASON SIRES

Expert Eye (Highest Timeform Rating **124**)

Acclamation – Exemplify (Dansili)

Expert Eye started odds on for the Dewhurst Stakes—such was the impression he made when impressively winning the Vintage Stakes at Goodwood on his previous outing—but he ultimately proved a big disappointment at Newmarket. He bounced back in no uncertain terms as a three-year-old, though, registering another clear-cut victory in the Jersey Stakes, outclassing Group 3 rivals again in the City of York Stakes later that summer and ending his career by coming out best in a bunched finish to the Breeders' Cup Mile. In proving himself effective in top company at up to a mile, Expert Eye therefore has a slightly different profile to Acclamation's other stallion sons who have been sprinters in the main. Dark Angel has been the most successful of those to date, while Acclamation's reputation as a sire of sires enjoyed another significant boost when Mehmas broke records on the way to becoming champion first-season sire in 2020. Joining the likes of Frankel and Kingman on Juddmonte's stallion roster, Expert Eye stood his first season at Banstead Manor at a fee of £20,000. Among his first book of mares were Juddmonte group winners Mirabilis, Tested and Treat Gently, while another of his offspring who'll be running in his breeders' colours is a half-sister to the Group 3-winning two-year-olds Brown Sugar and Burnt Sugar whom Juddmonte bought for 290,000 guineas at Tattersalls in October, making her his highest-priced yearling. With a first crop of around 100 foals, Expert Eye proved popular with commercial breeders as well having support from his own team, and he seems sure to make his presence felt.

Harry Angel (Ire) (Highest Timeform Rating **132**)

Dark Angel (Ire) – Beatrix Potter (Ire) (Cadeaux Genereux)

Not many horses lose their maiden status in a group race, but Harry Angel did just that when quickening away with the Mill Reef Stakes at Newbury on just his second start at two. That proved the prelude to a top-class sprinting career which brought him Group 1 success at three in the July Cup and Sprint Cup, his four-length win in soft ground at Haydock a top-drawer performance. Harry Angel proved just as good under firmer conditions, though, when carrying a penalty to success in the Duke of York Stakes on his reappearance at four in what proved a more frustrating campaign. Harry Angel's natural exuberance was part of what made him a top sprinter, but there was a downside to that aspect of his character as he tended to get upset in or around the stalls, twice suffering injuries from such incidents. A win at Ascot eluded him from

Harry Angel was a top-class sprinter on his day

several visits to the track, though his second place to Caravaggio (last year's champion first-season sire) in the Commonwealth Cup was a commendable performance on what was his first start in the Godolphin colours. The highest-rated son of Dark Angel to go to stud, Harry Angel's first crop was conceived at a fee of £20,000 at Dalham Hall. His most expensive yearling was a colt out of Red Box, a listed-winning daughter of the Prix de Diane winner Confidential Lady, who sold for £220,000 at Doncaster. Some speedy two-year-olds can be expected from Harry Angel's first crop of youngsters and it wouldn't surprise if there was a group winner among them.

Havana Grey (Highest Timeform Rating **118**)

Havana Gold (Ire) – Blanc de Chine (Ire) (Dark Angel (Ire))

Although he was by stamina influence Teofilo, Havana Gold proved a smart performer at up to a mile and the best of his offspring to date (sharing his Timeform rating with his sire, in fact), Havana Grey, proved even less typical of his sire-line. Instead, Havana Grey took after his useful dam Blanc de Chine, a daughter of Dark Angel who raced exclusively over five furlongs, and Havana Grey likewise proved best at the minimum trip, though he did finish second in the Prix Morny on his only try at six furlongs. He won four times as a two-year-old, notably the Molecomb Stakes at Goodwood, and trained on into a still better sprinter at three with wins at the Curragh in the Sapphire Stakes and Flying Five Stakes. In the latter contest, run for the first time as a Group 1, he had fellow first-season sire Sioux Nation (see below) just behind him in third. While one of the less expensive first-season sires (he stood for £8,000 at Whitsbury Manor in his first year at stud), the median price of his yearlings last year was £20,000. His most expensive yearling sold for £110,000 at Doncaster and is very speedily bred being out of an unraced half-sister to the Temple Stakes winner Pearl Secret and a half-brother to Ehraz, who was an impressive two-year-old winner over six furlongs at Ascot last year for Richard Hannon. Another with a first crop of around 100 foals, Havana Grey will almost certainly be one of the quickest first-season sires into his stride in 2022.

Sioux Nation (USA) (Highest Timeform Rating **117**)

Scat Daddy (USA) – Dream The Blues (Ire) (Oasis Dream)

Can Scat Daddy do it for Coolmore again? He's already been responsible for No Nay Never, champion first-season sire in 2018, and for Caravaggio, who took the same title last year when Cheveley Park Stakes winner Tenebrism was his best horse. No Nay Never and Caravaggio were both Royal Ascot winners as two-year-olds and so too was Sioux Nation, who emulated No Nay Never by winning the Norfolk Stakes. He followed that by winning the Phoenix Stakes, as Caravaggio had done a year earlier, and continued in that stablemate's footsteps again at three when winning the Lacken Stakes at Naas. Sioux Nation found life harder in the top sprints at three, but his fifth place to stable companion U S Navy Flag (see below) in the July Cup and third to Havana Grey in the Flying Five were other smart efforts. A big, good-bodied horse, Sioux Nation stood his first season at Coolmore at a fee of €12,500, his popularity such that he was the busiest first-season sire resulting in a huge crop of 142 foals. Notable among his yearlings to go through the ring were a half-sister to 1000 Guineas winner Mother Earth, who was sold for €230,000 to Al Shira'aa Farms at the Goffs Orby Sale, while Coolmore went to 215,000 guineas at Tattersalls in October for a colt out of the useful Irish sprinter Knock Stars. Weight of numbers alone puts Sioux Nation in pole position for his bid to join No Nay Never and Caravaggio as another champion first-season sire for Scat Daddy and Coolmore.

U S Navy Flag (USA) (Highest Timeform Rating **125**)

War Front (USA) – Misty For Me (Ire) (Galileo (Ire))

Sioux Nation isn't Coolmore's only sprinter with his first crop of two-year-olds to represent him in 2022. U S Navy Flag thrived on a busy campaign at two, particularly once blinkers were applied, winning the Middle Park Stakes and following up in the Dewhurst to become the first horse for 35 years to complete that double. Although runner-up in the Irish 2000 Guineas the following spring (his dam Misty For Me was an Irish 1000 Guineas winner), U S Navy Flag turned in his career-best effort when reverting to sprinting, making all to win a high-class edition of the July Cup. U S Navy Flag's opening fee was twice that of Sioux Nation and the median price of his yearlings was around £46,000. Some of his daughters sold particularly well, including a half-sister to smart US Grade 2 mile winner Going Global who was bought at the Orby Sale for €290,000, a half-sister to 2000 Guineas winner Poetic Flare who fetched €200,000 at the same venue and a filly out of Princess Elizabeth Stakes winner Epsom Icon who sold for €200,000 at Deauville in August. In keeping with his pedigree, U S Navy Flag was less of an out-and-out sprinter than Sioux Nation and there's no reason to think his first crop of two-year-olds will necessarily all be sprinters either. Another Coolmore-owned son of War Front who won the Dewhurst, Air Force Blue, has been moved on to South Korea after failing to set the world alight from his Kentucky base, but it will be disappointing if U S Navy Flag doesn't make more of an impact in Europe.

Zoustar (Aus) (Highest Timeform Rating **122+**)

Northern Meteor (Aus) – Zouzou (Aus) (Redoute's Choice (Aus))

Zoustar may be a first-season sire as far as the Northern Hemisphere is concerned, but he has plenty of 'form' already as a highly successful stallion in his native Australia. Indeed, he was champion first-season sire there in the 2017/18 season and the leading second-season stallion a year later. That's prompted his Australian stud fee to more than treble since starting at stud there, while his first British crop, as a result of shuttling to Qatar Racing's Tweenhill Stud, was conceived at a fee of £25,000 which, for context, was on a par with Cracksman's. Zoustar's most notable feat as a stallion down under was probably siring the first three in the Group 1 Coolmore Stakes over six furlongs at Flemington, a race which Zoustar had won himself; his other Group 1 win came in the Golden Rose Stakes over seven furlongs. Whilst principally a speedy type himself, it's worth noting that Zoustar's Galileo half-brothers Kondo Isami (a member of last year's *Fifty*) and the smart Emperor of The Sun, successful in Britain and Ireland respectively in 2021, are stayers. Zoustar's proven record as a stallion in Australia, rather than just his racing record there, no doubt helped him greatly when his first Northern Hemisphere yearlings went under the hammer; their median price was an impressive £52,500, with his most expensive yearling, a colt out of a sister to smart sprinter Royal Intervention, selling for 310,000 guineas at Tattersalls in October. His first runners in Britain and Ireland are awaited with interest.

Best of the rest

The stallions listed above are among those who can be expected to make the biggest impact with their first crop of two-year-olds. But there are other high-profile stallions who will be having their first runners in 2022. Among them is **Cracksman** (136), who is not only the highest-rated among the first-season sires of 2022, but he's also Frankel's best horse to date and the first of his sire's sons to embark on a stud career. Standing at Dalham Hall, Cracksman has a first crop of around 100 foals, which include a filly out of 1000 Guineas winner Speciosa, a half-brother to Al Kazeem and a half-brother to the dam of champion two-year-old Pinatubo. It will be fascinating, too, to see how the stallion careers of regular racecourse rivals **Roaring Lion** (130) and **Saxon Warrior** (124) get under way. The pair clashed on six occasions, with Saxon Warrior getting the better of their first two encounters in the Racing Post Trophy and 2000 Guineas before Roaring Lion gained the upper hand in the Eclipse, Juddmonte International and Irish Champion Stakes. Their other meeting came in the Derby in which Roaring Lion was third, a place ahead of Saxon Warrior. Sadly, Roaring Lion succumbed to colic in 2019 after siring his first crop, but his yearlings posted the highest median price, around £66,500, of any first-season sire. His top-priced yearling was a half-brother to Gold Cup winner Subjectivist who was bought by David Redvers for 450,000 guineas. Saxon Warrior, who started at Coolmore at a fee of €30,000, will be the first son of the late Japanese superstar stallion Deep Impact to have a sizeable crop of two-year-olds in Europe. They include a son of King's Stand Stakes winner Cassandra Go who sold for €540,000 at the Goffs Orby Sale. That makes him a half-brother to Halfway To Heaven, herself the dam of two more Ballydoyle Group 1-winning fillies, Magical and Rhododendron. This will be the first year that Galileo no longer figures on Coolmore's stallion roster, though they have several of his sons in residence and the latest one to have runners for the first time will be Superlative Stakes winner **Gustav Klimt** (123). Out of a sister/close relative to the highly successful stallions Kodiac and Invincible Spirit, Gustav Klimt was speedier than most by his sire, never racing beyond a mile and running one of his best races when third in the Sprint Cup. Finally, a couple of stallions with the right sort of profile to make their mark with speedy two-year-olds are **Kessaar** (113) and **Tasleet** (124). Kessaar, a son of Kodiac, was retired to stand alongside his sire at Tally-Ho Stud after a two-year-old season for John Gosden which brought him three wins, including in the Sirenia Stakes and Mill Reef Stakes. One to note from his first crop was a colt out of a half-sister to Flying Childers winner Ardad, himself a leading first-season sire in 2021, bought by Roger Varian for 90,000 guineas. As a gelding, there will be no stud career, of course, for the best sprinter of recent seasons, Battaash, who retired last year, but his relative Tasleet (their dams are half-sisters) was no mean sprinter himself. The son of Showcasing won the Duke of York Stakes as a four-year-old before finishing runner-up in the Diamond Jubilee, Sprint Cup and Champions Sprint later that season. Standing for just £6,000 in his first season at Nunnery Stud, Tasleet's top-priced yearling, a half-brother to smart Irish sprinter Gustavus Weston, sold for 80,000 guineas.

SECTION 4

TIMEFORM'S VIEW

Chosen from the Timeform Formbook, here is Timeform's detailed analysis—compiled by our team of race reporters and supplemented by observations from Timeform's handicappers—of a selection of key juvenile races from last year.

CURRAGH Sunday September 12

GOOD

Moyglare Stud Stakes (Group 1)

Pos	*Draw*	*Btn*	*Horse*	*Age*	*Wgt*	*Eq*	*Trainer*	*Jockey*	*SP*
1	8		DISCOVERIES (IRE)	2	9-2		Mrs J. Harrington, Ireland	Shane Foley	17/2
2	5	¾	AGARTHA (IRE)	2	9-2		Joseph P O'Brien, Ireland	Declan McDonogh	10/3
3	7	2	SUNSET SHIRAZ (IRE)	2	9-2		Gavin P Cromwell, Ireland	G. F. Carroll	12/1
4	6	1	CONCERT HALL (IRE)	2	9-2		Aidan O'Brien, Ireland	Seamie Heffernan	33/1
5	1	½	HOMELESS SONGS (IRE)	2	9-2		D. K. Weld, Ireland	Oisin James Orr	9/4
6	3	1¾	CAIRDE GO DEO (FR)	2	9-2		G. M. Lyons, Ireland	C. T. Keane	85/40f
7	4	nk	PRETTIEST (USA)	2	9-2		Aidan O'Brien, Ireland	Ryan Moore	14/1
8	2	10	MISSING MATRON (IRE)	2	9-2		J. S. Bolger, Ireland	K. J. Manning	150/1

8 ran Race Time 1m 27.10 Closing Sectional (3.00f): 35.55s (105.0%) Winning Owner: Niarchos Family

Not a particularly deep renewal of this Group 1 for fillies, Agartha the only one of them previously successful at listed level or higher, the market dominated by a pair of impressive last-time-out winners, but as is so often the case it was the Debutante form that proved key, the first 3 home in that race filling the same positions here, albeit not in quite the same order, Discoveries completing a memorable weekend for Jessica Harrington and Shane Foley. **Discoveries** was much improved to turn around Debutante form with Agartha, in doing so getting one over on her illustrious older siblings Alpha Centauri and Alpine Star by managing to win a Group 1 as a juvenile, a more aggressive ride doing the trick; close up, ridden 2f out, stayed on to lead final 100 yds; a tilt at the Breeders Cup Juvenile Fillies Turf, for which she is now qualified, is reportedly under consideration. **Agartha** the one to beat on form, didn't go down without a fight, deserving credit for consistency but hard to imagine there is much more to come from her; made running, tackled entering final 1f, headed final 100 yds, kept on. **Sunset Shiraz** backed up previous effort to confirm herself useful, surely just a matter of time until she sheds her maiden tag; held up, headway over 2f out, driven over 1f out, edged right, kept on. **Concert Hall** ran well on form without ever looking like winning, her performance one of late gains; waited with, forced wide 2f out, kept on, never nearer; will stay at least 1m. **Homeless Songs** well supported on the back of an impressive debut win (beat Agartha), failed to do herself justice, still in need of the experience; mid-division, raced freely, switched soon after halfway, effort 2f out, held when carried right final 1f, no extra; she showed up well for a long way despite doing too much early on and remains one to be positive about. **Cairde Go Deo** strong in the betting, failed to meet expectations, something presumably not right and Colin Keane quick to accept the situation; chased leaders, travelled well, shaken up under 2f out, found less than looked likely, not persevered with once held. **Prettiest** isn't up to this grade; held up, kept on, never landed a blow. **Missing Matron** without the headgear this time, was out of her depth; chased leaders, driven 3f out, weakened.

Goffs Vincent O'Brien National Stakes (Group 1)

Pos	Draw	Btn	Horse	Age	Wgt	Eq	Trainer	Jockey	SP
1	7		NATIVE TRAIL	2	9-5		Charlie Appleby	William Buick	7/2
2	1	3½	POINT LONSDALE (IRE)	2	9-5		Aidan O'Brien, Ireland	Ryan Moore	8/13f
3	4	½	EBRO RIVER (IRE)	2	9-5		Hugo Palmer	James Doyle	13/2
4	5	2¼	ULTRAMARINE (IRE)	2	9-5		Joseph P O'Brien, Ireland	S. M. Crosse	100/1
5	2	nk	GREAT MAX (IRE)	2	9-5		Michael Bell	Rossa Ryan	28/1
6	6	3¾	DUKE DE SESSA (IRE)	2	9-5		D. K. Weld, Ireland	C. T. Keane	8/1
7	3	8½	ANATOLI	2	9-5		J. J. Feane, Ireland	K. J. Manning	125/1

7 ran Race Time 1m 26.27 Closing Sectional (3.00f): 35.90s (103.0%) Winning Owner: Godolphin

The premier 2-y-o race of the season in Ireland went the way of the Appelby/Buick/Godolphin combination for the third time in 4 years, Native Trail producing a very smart performance to lower the colours of the hitherto unbeaten Point Lonsdale in what was a truly run affair. **Native Trail** is improving in leaps and bounds despite the fact that he is clearly learning on the job, taking his record to 3 from 3 to emulate connections' Quorto in completing the Superlative/National Stakes double, looking a high-class prospect as he ran right away from Point Lonsdale in the final 1f; mid-division, shaken up 2f out, ran green, led last ½f, forged clear; he's reportedly being aimed at the Dewhurst, sure to take all the beating there. **Point Lonsdale** lost his unbeaten record, simply second best on the day, having no answer to the winner's turn of foot; pressed leader, pushed along 2f out, every chance well inside final 1f, left behind by winner final 100 yds; he's crying out for a step up in trip and remains open to improvement with that in mind. **Ebro River** back at the scene of his Phoenix Stakes win, proved there was no fluke about that, impressing with how he travelled through the race only for his stamina to ebb away late on; made running, travelled well, tackled entering final 1f, headed well inside final 1f, no extra. **Ultramarine** progressed again to make the frame in pattern company for the second consecutive start; mid-division, headway 2f out, not clear run over 1f out, kept on. **Great Max** ran about as well as could have been expected upped in grade; chased leaders, driven over 2f out, faded. **Duke de Sessa** failed to build on the promise of last run, this coming a bit too early in his development; held up, ridden over 2f out, not persevered with once held, made no impression; should still improve. **Anatoli** making turf debut, wasn't up to the task; always behind.

NEWMARKET (ROWLEY) Saturday September 25

GOOD to FIRM

Juddmonte Cheveley Park Stakes (Group 1) (1)

Pos	Draw	Btn	Horse	Age	Wgt	Eq	Trainer	Jockey	SP
1	11		TENEBRISM (USA)	2	9-0		Aidan O'Brien, Ireland	Ryan Moore	14/1
2	13	1	FLOTUS (IRE)	2	9-0		Simon & Ed Crisford	James Doyle	11/1
3	2	3	SANDRINE	2	9-0		Andrew Balding	David Probert	3/1
4	12	¾	GUILDED (IRE)	2	9-0		K. R. Burke	Clifford Lee	100/1
5	5	nk	DESERT DREAMER	2	9-0	(t)	Stuart Williams	Oisin Murphy	14/1
6	9	1¾	ILLUSTRATING	2	9-0		K. R. Burke	Daniel Tudhope	25/1
7	7	¾	HAVE A GOOD DAY (IRE)	2	9-0		Florian Guyader, France	Maxime Guyon	40/1
8	3	¾	SACRED BRIDGE	2	9-0		G. M. Lyons, Ireland	C. T. Keane	13/8f
9	10	¾	EVE LODGE	2	9-0		Charlie Fellowes	Jamie Spencer	50/1
10	1	½	ZAIN CLAUDETTE (IRE)	2	9-0		Ismail Mohammed	Ray Dawson	6/1

11	4	½	CORAZON (IRE)	2	9-0	George Boughey	William Buick	28/1
12	8	5½	THUNDER LOVE	2	9-0	George Boughey	Rossa Ryan	50/1

12 ran Race Time 1m 11.00 Closing Sectional (3.00f): 34.40s (103.2%) Winning Owner: Westerberg/Coolmore/Merribelle Stables

In many ways a typical Cheveley Park, with so many of the best fillies 2-y-o form lines represented, 11 of the 12 having run in pattern races and with at least 4 runs under their belt, Tenebrism the one exception, not seen since a winning debut in March, the first to win this race off just one run since Regal Rose in 2000, her form looking among the better performances in this race in recent years, the time comparing very favourably with that for the Middle Park, the one concern about the form the advantage that those racing near the stand side rail had, the runner-up and fourth, who raced there along with the winner, both appearing to improve a fair bit for that. **Tenebrism** produced a remarkable performance on just her second start, off since the opening day of the season in Ireland, producing a really strong finish to deny the runner-up, that she had an advantage in racing against the rail likely, not that that should take much away from what was a rare win for one so inexperienced in this race; slowly into stride, raced off the pace, shaken up halfway, headway approaching final 1f, found plenty to lead final 50 yds; although her sire isn't yet looking much of an influence for stamina, the dam's side of her pedigree encourages obvious thoughts of the Guineas, a chance that she will have another run before the year is over anyway, though all in all she's an exciting prospect, potentially out of the top drawer. **Flotus** progressed again, as expected making more impact at this level with Ripon behind her, finally now fulfilling the promise of her debut, though at the very least she was seen to maximum advantage, close to the stand rail, having all those racing wider in trouble a fair way out, just denied by a potentially top-class filly; broke well, led, went with zest, quickened 2f out, ridden final 1f, kept on, worn down final 50 yds; she's raced at up to 6f, her pedigree offering mixed signals so far as longer distances are concerned, though presumably the Fred Darling will be under consideration as a starting point in the spring. **Sandrine** ran creditably, kept to 6f, doing best of those away from the favoured rail and deserving marking up for that; a race like the Fred Darling presumably on the agenda for the spring, no reason why connections shouldn't still have Guineas ambitions with her; held up, headway 2f out, chased leader approaching final 1f, one paced. **Guilded** quickly turned out after picking up a soft option at Beverley in the week, ran her best race, though she was close to the favoured rail and there is obviously a chance she is flattered; chased leader, ridden over 2f out, not quicken approaching final 1f. **Desert Dreamer** in first-time tongue strap, is running consistently well at pattern level, without getting her head in front, plenty to like about her effort from the wrong part of the track here; held up, travelled well, good headway over 1f out, not quicken well inside final 1f. **Illustrating** wasn't disgraced, facing a stiff task in this grade, signs that she will benefit from the longer trip at a more realistic level; waited with, shaken up over 2f out, not quicken, plugged on final 1f. **Have A Good Day** was up against it at this level and never really looked likely to get involved; held up, effort over 2f out, made no impression. **Sacred Bridge** looked the pick on the form she showed in winning the Round Tower last time, following the same route as her stable's Lightening Pearl, who won this in 2011, unable to repeat the feat and a fair way below that form, her response when shaken up suggesting she might have been past her best for the year; in touch, travelled well, chased leaders halfway, shaken up 2f out, not quicken, no extra late on. **Eve Lodge** had had her Sirenia form boosted the previous weekend, but this was a tougher task back on turf and she just wasn't in the same form; in touch, shaken up halfway, not quicken, badly hampered under 2f out, lost place. **Zain Claudette** had form lines that tied her in with the third and fifth, but she wasn't able to run to that level, with the worst of the draw, though the third came from the stall next to her, just likely that she was past her best for the year (connections blamed the ground as unsuitable 'on this occasion', even though she'd run on nothing else and been doing very well); waited with, ridden over 2f out, not quicken, weakened inside final 1f. **Corazon** was well below form, caught on the wrong side of the field, beaten before the longer trip came into play; in touch, ridden over 2f out, not quicken, weakened inside final 1f. **Thunder Love** was back to being ridden prominently and she failed to confirm the improved form she'd shown in the Flying Childers, not really handling the track either, the longer trip not the issue; chased leader, ridden over 2f out, hung right, lost place soon after.

Juddmonte Middle Park Stakes (Group 1) (1)

Pos	*Draw*	*Btn*	*Horse*	*Age*	*Wgt*	*Eq*	*Trainer*	*Jockey*	*SP*
1	1		PERFECT POWER (IRE)	2	9-0		Richard Fahey	Christophe Soumillon	11/4f
2	2	½	CASTLE STAR (IRE)	2	9-0		J. A. Stack, Ireland	Jamie Spencer	12/1
3	8	nk	ARMOR	2	9-0		Richard Hannon	Pat Dobbs	9/1
4	4	nk	GO BEARS GO (IRE)	2	9-0		David Loughnane	Rossa Ryan	7/2
5	7	nk	TWILIGHT JET (IRE)	2	9-0		M. D. O'Callaghan, Ireland	L. F. Roche	28/1
5	5	dh	CATURRA (IRE)	2	9-0		Clive Cox	Adam Kirby	12/1
7	9	½	ASYMMETRIC (IRE)	2	9-0		Alan King	Martin Harley	17/2
8	10	¾	DR ZEMPF	2	9-0		G. M. Lyons, Ireland	C. T. Keane	9/2
9	6	1¾	NEW YORK CITY (IRE)	2	9-0		Aidan O'Brien, Ireland	W. M. Lordan	33/1
10	3	10	HMS ENDEAVOUR (USA)	2	9-0		Aidan O'Brien, Ireland	Ryan Moore	14/1

10 ran Race Time 1m 11.32 Closing Sectional (3.00f): 35.00s (101.9%) Winning Owner: Sheikh Rashid Dalmook Al Maktoum

After the Cheveley Park had shown a seemingly obvious advantage to racing against the near rail, everyone wanted to be there in this, which made for a messy race, several finding trouble in running, including the second and third, the winner not going so well as that pair but finding a clear route and ultimately winning with a bit to spare, though with barely 2 lengths covering the first 8 and the time slower than for the Cheveley Park, it's hard to take a particularly positive view of the form, the winner's effort not any better than the one he produced to win the Morny, an average one for this race at best, too many of the 8 in a heap already appearing no more than useful coming into the race. **Perfect Power** added a second Group 1 to his tally, given a lovely ride that removed as much as possible the chance of trouble, a trap the placed runners fell into, though such was the way he crossed the line that it would be a stretch to say he was lucky at all; held up, shaken up over 2f out, headway over 1f out, led last ½f, kept on, had bit in hand; he may well prove to be a sprinter, though, given the stamina on the dam's side of the pedigree, it would presumably appeal to connections to give a shot at the Guineas in the spring. **Castle Star** emerged best of the 4 that contested the Phoenix Stakes (a shame the winner Ebro River didn't take his chance here), given a classic Spencer ride, running really well, though with a sense that he might have done even better, given he was going better than the winner 2f out, the pair side by side at the back of the field; steadied at the start, held up, travelled well, switched soon after start, hampered over 1f out, shaken up after, kept on inside final 1f, took second final 50 yds; he holds an entry in the Irish Guineas, though he wouldn't be sure to stay more than 7f and his record suggests even that would be a stretch. **Armor** clearly doesn't need soft ground to run to the level he did at Goodwood, matching that effort, holding the advantage of the rail for a long way, but forced to make his move away from it and having to weave through; held up, travelled well, headway under 2f out, short of room entering final 1f, ridden, ran on; he's been campaigned as a sprinter, though there are elements in his pedigree which suggest he could be tried over further next year. **Go Bears Go** emerged only second best of the quartet that contested the Phoenix Stakes, but he ran up to his best, sticking to his task well, suggesting he'd be worth a try at 7f, though he looks more a sprinter and was on his toes beforehand as well; disputed lead until halfway, shaken up after, not quicken over 1f out, kept on again final 100 yds. **Twilight Jet** ran well, though given the right ride, more forcefully ridden over this shorter trip and able to bag the rail, that enabling him to hold the lead until very late in the day; led, travelled well, shaken up over 1f out, kept on, headed final ½f, weakened close home. **Caturra** proved at least as good as previously, returned to 6f, continuing to stand up well to a busy campaign, very much a 2-y-o on looks; chased leaders, ridden over 2f out, outpaced briefly, every chance well inside final 1f, no extra close home. **Asymmetric** ran his race, a smidgin further behind the winner than he had been in the Morny, looking pretty exposed as no more than useful and lacking the scope of some of the others for next year; held up, took keen hold, shaken up 2f out, headway over 1f out, every chance briefly well inside final 1f, no extra close home. **Dr Zempf** ran respectably, though given his draw and track position he might have been expected to do even better; chased leader, ridden over 2f out, not quicken. **New York City** was thrown in at the deep end and acquitted himself as well as could be expected, plenty to like about him physically, a proper sprint type on looks, and every chance he could develop further next year; chased leaders, shaken up 2f out, not quicken, faded inside final 1f; open to further improvement. **Hms Endeavour** slightly the more fancied of the 2 O'Brien runners and with Moore on board, just ran no sort of race, in trouble a long way out; waited with, shaken up halfway, dropped away under 2f out; he's got more scope than most of these, not an obvious sprinter on looks, and he may yet do better.

NEWMARKET (ROWLEY) Friday October 8

GOOD to SOFT

Bet365 Fillies' Mile (Group 1) (1)

Pos	*Draw*	*Btn*	*Horse*	*Age*	*Wgt*	*Eq*	*Trainer*	*Jockey*	*SP*
1	8		INSPIRAL	2	9-0		John & Thady Gosden	Frankie Dettori	8/11f
2	7	2½	PROSPEROUS VOYAGE (IRE)	2	9-0		Ralph Beckett	Rob Hornby	16/1
3	9	nk	CACHET (IRE)	2	9-0		George Boughey	James Doyle	22/1
4	2	sh	MISE EN SCENE	2	9-0		James Ferguson	Cieren Fallon	15/2
5	4	½	WILD BEAUTY	2	9-0		Charlie Appleby	William Buick	15/2
6	3	¾	CONCERT HALL (IRE)	2	9-0		Aidan O'Brien, Ireland	Ryan Moore	17/2
7	6	1¼	MAGICAL LAGOON (IRE)	2	9-0		Mrs J. Harrington, Ireland	Shane Foley	20/1

8	5	2½	BOUQUET	2	9-0	John & Thady Gosden	Robert Havlin	22/1
9	1	¾	MAJESTIC GLORY	2	9-0	Andrew Balding	David Probert	25/1

9 ran Race Time 1m 38.44 Closing Sectional (3.00f): 36.45s (101.3%) Winning Owner: Cheveley Park Stud

The 2-y-o fillies hadn't looked a vintage bunch for much of the campaign, but the Fillies' Mile followed the Cheveley Park in showcasing the ability of one likely to be a major player in next year's classics, Inspiral justifying her short price with a thoroughly convincing victory, the form perhaps not so good as that in the Cheveley Park, the race a little short on depth compared to some years and the winner's performance no more than average for the race, though there is a fair bit more to come; the third and winner raced apart from the other runners in the centre, the runner-up having taken the main group over to the far rail, the field converging over 2f out. **Inspiral** completed a perfect campaign with a dominant victory in the top race for staying 2-y-o fillies, a lot to like about the way she moved into contention, that she needed her mind made up before she stamped her full authority on the race not really a concern, her record making her a strong contender for classic honours next year, this form not looking quite so good as Tenebrism showed in the Cheveley Park, though both fillies are only just scratching the surface of what they can do; patiently ridden behind leader in centre, travelled strongly, good headway over 2f out, led soon after, ridden over 1f out, kept on well inside final 1f, well on top finish; an exciting prospect for 2022. **Prosperous Voyage** chased home Inspiral again, just as she had in the May Hill, this better form in a deeper race; soon led, shaken up over 2f out, headed soon after, not quicken over 1f out, kept on close home; she is half-sister to middle-distance winners and her maiden brother stays 11.5f, so there's every chance she will proved at least as effective when she steps up in trip next year. **Cachet** fully confirmed her improved effort in the Rockfel, following the third that day Oscula in paying a compliment to the winner Hello You, though she was again well positioned and probably seen to best advantage; led pair in centre, shaken up and every chance 2f out, left behind by winner from over 1f out, not quicken and lost second well inside final 1f; she's by some way the best runner so far in Britain and Ireland from the first crop of Aclaim, showing rather more stamina than a lot of his progeny, her dam's side suggesting she could well stay beyond 1m. **Mise En Scene** on softer ground than previously, lost her unbeaten record, running at least as well as at Goodwood, but seeming still a little short on experience, not really finding her stride until it was too late; held up, took keen hold, labouring under 3f out, stayed on entering final 1f, nearest at the finish; she remains capable of better. **Wild Beauty** ran to a useful level, probably about as well as she had when winning in Canada the time before, well positioned and seemingly beaten fair and square; close up, shaken up 3f out, not quicken under 2f out, hung left, plugged on. **Concert Hall** ran creditably without finding any improvement stepped up to 1m, the way she shapes and her pedigree both suggesting that this trip and further will show her to advantage next year, that her stable's beaten runners in this race in recent years include Mother Earth, Snowfall, Love and Magical more than enough reason to remain positive about her longer-term prospects; led early, in touch after, outpaced soon after halfway, kept on again final 1f. **Magical Lagoon** was essentially found out in better company, this a fair bit stronger than the Group 3 she won at the Curragh, though she possibly didn't handle the track that well either; tracked pace, shaken up over 3f out, lost place over 2f out; she's not really bred to be a leading 2-y-o, a well-made filly with a middle-distance pedigree—her winning half-siblings including the King George winner Novellist—and she could well come into her own once stepped up in trip at 3 yrs. **Bouquet** had plenty of improvement to make to figure in this higher grade and she wasn't up to the task at this stage of her career, still a bit green and never a factor; slowly into stride, raced off the pace, ridden over 3f out, not quicken, left behind over 1f out; she has plenty of substance to her physically and may yet do better at 3 yrs, at this stage looking likely to take after the stouter dam's side of her pedigree. **Majestic Glory** over an extra 1f, was back on easier ground, but fared little better than she had in the Rockfel, her campaign rather tailing off, perhaps just past her best for the year the last twice; settled in touch, ridden under 3f out, not quicken, dropped away final 1f.

NEWMARKET (ROWLEY) Saturday October 9
GOOD to SOFT

Darley Dewhurst Stakes (Group 1) (1)

Pos	Draw	Btn	Horse	Age	Wgt	Eq	Trainer	Jockey	SP
1	5		NATIVE TRAIL	2	9-1		Charlie Appleby	William Buick	5/6f
2	6	2	DUBAWI LEGEND (IRE)	2	9-1		Hugo Palmer	James Doyle	12/1
3	7	½	BAYSIDE BOY (IRE)	2	9-1		Roger Varian	David Egan	9/1
4	3	1¾	BERKSHIRE SHADOW	2	9-1	(t)	Andrew Balding	Oisin Murphy	22/1
5	1	2	DHABAB (IRE)	2	9-1		John & Thady Gosden	Frankie Dettori	12/1
6	4	½	GLOUNTHAUNE (IRE)	2	9-1		Aidan O'Brien, Ireland	Ryan Moore	20/1
7	2	¾	GO BEARS GO (IRE)	2	9-1		David Loughnane	Rossa Ryan	11/1
8	8	½	STRAIGHT ANSWER	2	9-1	(t)	G. M. Lyons, Ireland	C. T. Keane	6/1

8 ran Race Time 1m 24.82 Closing Sectional (3.00f): 35.05s (103.7%) Winning Owner: Godolphin

So often the decisive race in determining the top 2-y-o of the year, this renewal likely to be no different, allowing that the Futurity is among the races still to come, Native Trail already with form good enough to win an average running, not needing to better that against slightly weaker opposition than he'd faced at the Curragh, again his strength in the finish the key to his performance, fascinating to compare him with his stable-companion Coroebus in the Autumn Stakes earlier on the card, both earmarked for the Guineas in the spring, the last 5 winners of the Dewhurst all successful at Group 1 level again subsequently, though only the first of those, Churchill, in 2016, went on to win the Guineas back here; the field, for the first time over the 2 days, came right to the stand rail, a chance that that showed the runner-up to advantage, given how often it's been favoured in recent years, though he's been given full credit for his improved performance for now. **Native Trail** stood out on form and didn't need to improve further to gain a second win at this level, the best 2-y-o colt this year so far, a strapping physique which promises much for next year, the one concerning thing about him is that he doesn't travel as one would expect from his pretty speedy pedigree, almost the first off the bridle but strong from 2f out to wear down the leader; waited with, shaken up soon after halfway, switched over 1f out, stayed on to lead well inside final 1f, in command soon after, well on top finish; he shapes as if he will be at least as effective at 1m, even if that isn't so obvious from his pedigree, and the Guineas is the obvious target for next spring. **Dubawi Legend** had had his big reputation dented in the Acomb, but showed it to be justified with a much-improved effort, a chance that he was at an advantage near the rail, but given full credit for now, plenty to like about his performance, getting all in trouble when he pressed on and overhauled only by the winner late on, every chance that he will progress again, a trip to the US an option later this autumn; close up, travelled well, led after 3f, shaken up 2f out, kept on, headed well inside final 1f, one paced; he's bred to be suited by 1m+. **Bayside Boy** confirmed himself a smart 2-y-o in a much more satisfactory race than at Doncaster, taking a while to find his stride when asked, possibly due to the track, but seeing things out well, even if no threat to the first 2; held up, effort 2f out, hung right, stayed on inside final 1f, nearest at the finish; he will stay at least 1m. **Berkshire Shadow** in first-time tongue strap, ran a good deal better than when favourite for the Gimcrack, more at home back at 7f, this at least as well as he's ever run; held up, effort over 2f out, stayed on approaching final 1f, never on terms; he's likely to stay 1m, which will make him easier to place at 3 yrs. **Dhabab** was an optimistic runner at this level, shorter in the market than he ought to have been, and he ran as well as could be expected, just not up to this grade, back at 7f; waited with, took keen hold, shaken up over 2f out, no extra over 1f out; he's probably not going to be easy to place next year. **Glounthaune** was the sole representative of a stable that has such a good record in this race and had a similar profile to the Cheveley Park winner (not seen since an impressive winning debut very early in the season), but he appeared unfancied and ran as if the experience was still needed, running to a useful level nevertheless and a real scopey sort who should come into his own at 3 yrs; stumbled start, waited with, shaken up over 2f out, ran green, weakened under 2f out; he's entered in the Irish 2000 Guineas, 7f/1m likely to be the sort of trip he'll start off at next year. **Go Bears Go** was below form for the first time in his career, and though he'd looked worth a try at 7f in the Middle Park, it didn't come off, lack of stamina likely to have been a factor, as well as just not being in quite the same form as previously; chased leaders, took keen hold, shaken up over 2f out, weakened over 1f out. **Straight Answer** had looked a potential top-notcher in winning at listed level last time, so he was rather disappointing facing a much tougher assignment less than 3 weeks later, beaten before the longer trip came into play (should stay 7f); led 3f, chased leader after, weakened over 1f out; given the good impression he'd created in winning his first 2 starts, he could well bounce back next spring.

DONCASTER Saturday October 23

HEAVY

Vertem Futurity Trophy Stakes (Group 1) (1)

Pos	Draw	Btn	Horse	Age	Wgt	Eq	Trainer	Jockey	SP
1	2		LUXEMBOURG (IRE)	2	9-1		Aidan O'Brien, Ireland	Ryan Moore	4/6f
2	1	1¾	SISSOKO (IRE)	2	9-1		Donnacha A O'Brien, Ireland	W. M. Lordan	9/1
3	6	sh	BAYSIDE BOY (IRE)	2	9-1		Roger Varian	David Egan	9/2
4	4	hd	HANNIBAL BARCA (IRE)	2	9-1		Brian Meehan	Paul Mulrennan	25/1
5	5	½	IMPERIAL FIGHTER (IRE)	2	9-1		Andrew Balding	David Probert	11/1
6	3	10	MCTIGUE (IRE)	2	9-1		J. S. Bolger, Ireland	R. P. Cleary	33/1
7	8	3	BULLET FORCE (IRE)	2	9-1		K. R. Burke	Rossa Ryan	100/1
8	7	1½	ROYAL PATRONAGE (FR)	2	9-1		Mark Johnston	Jason Hart	7/1

8 ran Race Time 1m 43.64 Closing Sectional (2.00f): 25.10s (103.2%) Winning Owner: Westerberg/Mrs J Magnier/M Tabor/D Smith

A record-equalling tenth win for Aidan O'Brien in a race with a rich history of producing classic winners and Luxembourg looks a worthy successor to some of his stable's previous winners, even if the bare form on the day can't be rated too highly, with the next wave of finishers in a heap behind a winner who asserted with no small degree of comfort. **Luxembourg** maintained his unbeaten record, not needing to improve but essentially a ready winner, getting to the front easily and doing no more than required once there, behind only Native Trail among the season's juveniles and as likely a Derby winner as has been seen out so far (sure to be suited by middle distances), though the Guineas could be on the agenda first, and his stable's last 2 winners of this (Magna Grecia and Saxon Warrior) have landed that classic; mid-division, good headway over 2f out, led approaching final 1f, in command after, ridden out. **Sissoko** has come a long way in little time, running a fine race to place in a Group 1 just 9 days on from his maiden win and less than a month after his debut; close up, challenged over 2f out, no match for winner but kept on to edge second; it's easy to see him doing better still and he's sure to be suited by at least 1¼m as a 3-y-o. **Bayside Boy** ran another sound race at the top level, a bit better than the result considering he didn't have the clearest run through; dwelt, held up, short of room over 2f out, headway over 1f out, chased leaders final 1f, kept on, seeing out the longer trip well; he'll stay 1¼m. **Hannibal Barca** has had his Salisbury win well franked and was much improved to make the frame up in grade, starting his effort from last and sticking at it; in rear, headway 2f out, kept on; a long-striding galloper, he'll stay at least 1¼m and has the makings of an even better 3-y-o. **Imperial Fighter** ran as well as he had when second in the Autumn Stakes, having his chance and needing no excuses; in touch, pushed along over 2f out, kept on. **Mctigue** after 11 weeks off, wasn't up to this better company; bumped start, close up, ridden over 2f out, lost place. **Bullet Force** was out of depth; mid-division, left behind under 2f out. **Royal Patronage** on softer ground than previously, dropped away as if amiss and was later said to have been struck into; led until under 2f out, weakened final 1f; this doesn't undo the good work he's done this season and he's got the scope to train on, plus enough stamina in his pedigree to think 1¼m+ will be no problem.

BEST OF 2021 IN EUROPE

Juveniles

For the second time in three years, Charlie Appleby and Godolphin were responsible for Timeform's highest-rated two-year-old in Europe. Admittedly, **Native Trail** (122p) didn't reach anything like the same heights as Pinatubo two years earlier in pure form terms but, like that horse, he went into winter quarters unbeaten with a pair of Group 1 wins in the National Stakes at the Curragh and the Dewhurst Stakes at Newmarket on his CV. He was particularly impressive when successful at the Curragh, forging clear late on to beat the hitherto unbeaten **Point Lonsdale** (114p) by three and a half lengths, and it was a case of job done at Newmarket as he didn't need to be at his very best to land the spoils by two lengths from **Dubawi Legend** (114).

Native Trail rightfully heads the ante-post betting for the 2000 Guineas, a race in which the main danger could prove to be his stablemate **Coroebus** (116p), an impressive two-length winner of the Autumn Stakes at Newmarket on his final start. Native Trail

Native Trail was Timeform's highest-rated two-year-old in 2021

and Coroebus both have the scope to train on well as three-year-olds and they promise to give Appleby a very strong hand as he seeks a first success in the opening classic of the season, along with the progressive **Modern Games** (115), who completed a hat-trick with victory in the Breeders' Cup Juvenile Turf at Del Mar.

Perfect Power (114) was the pick of the sprinting two-year-olds as he registered back-to-back Group 1 wins in the Prix Morny at Deauville and the Middle Park Stakes at Newmarket. A representative field went to post on the last occasion with the exception of the Phoenix Stakes winner **Ebro River** (113), who appeared unsuited by the emphasis on stamina when last seen finishing down the field behind **Angel Bleu** (114) in the Prix Jean-Luc Lagardere at Longchamp. Angel Bleu went on to match Perfect Power's achievement by doubling his Group 1 tally with a hard-fought defeat of **Ancient Rome** (113) in the Criterium International at Saint-Cloud, the same card on which **El Bodegon** (111) gave James Ferguson the biggest success of his fledgling training career so far in the Criterium de Saint-Cloud.

Aidan O'Brien plundered two big two-year-old races in the space of 10 minutes when **Luxembourg** (118p) won the Beresford Stakes at the Curragh and **Tenebrism** (115p) won the Cheveley Park Stakes at Newmarket. A hugely exciting prospect, Luxembourg later maintained his unbeaten record in the Futurity Trophy at Doncaster, just needing to be nudged out to beat **Sissoko** (111) by a length and three quarters. Back in third was **Bayside Boy** (113) who provided substance to the form given that he had previously won the Champagne Stakes on Town Moor—beating the wide-margin Solario Stakes winner **Reach For The Moon** (113) by a head—before also finishing third in the Dewhurst.

Tenebrism was Timeform's highest-rated two-year-old filly in Europe after her Cheveley Park success, producing a remarkable performance to beat **Flotus** (111) by a length, particularly as it was her first start since making a winning debut on the opening day of the turf season in Ireland. She is sure to be aimed at the 1000 Guineas in the spring, putting her on a collision course with the Fillies' Mile winner **Inspiral** (112p), who is currently favoured in the ante-post betting. Inspiral was well on top at the finish when maintaining her unbeaten record at Newmarket, while Prix Marcel Boussac winner **Zellie** (111p) and Moyglare Stud Stakes winner **Discoveries** (107p) also struck at the top level to put themselves in contention for top honours in 2022.

Sprinters

Timeform's highest-rated sprinter for the fourth year in a row in 2020, **Battaash** (121+) was back for more during the latest season, but it quickly became apparent that he was no longer the force of old and he was retired after finishing only seventh in the King George Stakes at Goodwood, a race he won every year between 2017 and 2020. That left everything to play for in this division and, in Battaash's absence, the remaining sprinters proved much of a muchness with no horse managing to win at the top level more than once.

It might have been a different story but for the injury to **Dream of Dreams** (125) which kept him on the sidelines after his victory in the Diamond Jubilee Stakes at Royal Ascot. That was the second Group 1 success of his career—he also won the Sprint Cup in 2020—and it was a race he thoroughly deserved to win after finding one too good in the two previous editions, timing his challenge perfectly this time to overhaul **Glen Shiel** (119) and **Art Power** (121) inside the final furlong. Dream of Dreams will be back in 2022 with a clean bill of health, a comment which also applies to **Oxted** (123), who had surgery for a leg injury after finishing third in the July Cup at Newmarket. Oxted had previously shown very smart form to win the King's Stand Stakes at Royal Ascot, benefiting from a pace collapse back at the minimum trip as he finished best of all to get the verdict by a length and three quarters.

Elsewhere at Royal Ascot, **Rohaan** (121) produced the performance of a Group 1 sprinter to defy a BHA mark of 112 in the Wokingham Stakes, while the fate of the Commonwealth Cup was decided in dramatic circumstances. The Wesley Ward-trained filly **Campanelle** (117) was carried right in the final furlong by **Dragon Symbol** (122)

Starman produced a high-class performance to win the July Cup

and, after passing the post just a head behind that rival, she was eventually awarded the race by the stewards. Like Rohaan, **Creative Force** (123) was ineligible to run in the Commonwealth Cup as a gelding, but he was still amongst the winners at Royal Ascot, taking the step up to seven furlongs in his stride with an authoritative victory in the Jersey Stakes. Creative Force briefly found his progress stalling after that win, but that all changed in the Champions Sprint Stakes back at Ascot in which he produced a career-best effort to make the breakthrough in Group 1 company. A notable absentee at Ascot was **Starman** (125), who achieved as high a rating as any of the six-furlong sprinters when winning the July Cup in impressive fashion. However, he failed to repeat that effort in two subsequent starts at the top level, finishing third to **Marianafoot** (122) in the Prix Maurice de Gheest at Deauville and second to **Emaraaty Ana** (120) in the Sprint Cup at Haydock.

The French-trained **Suesa** (125) produced the best five-furlong performance in Europe when winning the King George Stakes by three lengths, teeing up a fascinating clash with the US raider **Golden Pal** (126) in the Nunthorpe Stakes at York. In the event, however, they were both upstaged by the local runner **Winter Power** (123), who showed bundles of speed to become the first three-year-old winner of the race since 2011. Golden Pal was a big disappointment on the Knavesmire, but he showed his true colours back on home soil when winning the Breeders' Cup Turf Sprint at Del Mar, looking a match for any of these if returning to Europe in 2022. By contrast, Winter Power went downhill after the Nunthorpe, finishing down the field in the Flying Five Stakes at the Curragh and the Prix de l'Abbaye at Longchamp, both races won by Irish-trained sprinters. **Romantic Proposal** (116) came out on top at the Curragh before the runner-up in that race, **A Case of You** (121), enjoyed his day in the sun with a narrow victory at Longchamp.

Milers

The Queen Elizabeth II Stakes at Ascot treated us to a thrilling clash of the generations. In the one corner there was the outstanding four-year-old miler **Palace Pier** (129), who had already won the Lockinge Stakes at Newbury, the Queen Anne Stakes at Royal Ascot and the Prix Jacques le Marois at Deauville (for the second year in a row) in 2021. In the other corner there was the unbeaten three-year-old **Baaeed** (130), who had made giant strides in a career spanning five starts in the space of just three months, culminating with a first Group 1 success in the Prix du Moulin de Longchamp.

In the event, the race lived up to expectations with Baaeed the winner fair and square, quickening to lead over a furlong out and always doing enough from there to win by a neck from Palace Pier, leaving the very smart mare **Lady Bowthorpe** (120) and the 2020 winner **The Revenant** (125) to complete the frame. Palace Pier

Baaeed (second right) edges out Palace Pier in the QEII

has since been retired to stud, leaving the top-class Baaeed as very much the one to beat in this division as a four-year-old, though he also has the option of going up in trip (bred to stay at least another two furlongs). Incidentally, Baaeed's trainer William Haggas could have a second string to his bow in this division in 2022 as **Aldaary** (124) ran to a high rating when defying a BHA mark of 109 in the Balmoral Handicap on the same card.

Poetic Flare (127) was comfortably the pick of the other three-year-old milers, thriving during a busy campaign which took in the 2000 Guineas and both the French and Irish equivalents. He registered his first success at the top level when getting the verdict in a very tight finish at Newmarket, digging deep to beat **Master of The Seas** (122) and **Lucky Vega** (121) by a short head and a neck. It was hard to take a high view of that form given the fine margins involved, but there was much better to come from Poetic Flare when he won the St James's Palace Stakes at Royal Ascot by four and a quarter lengths, the widest winning margin in that race in the last 30 years. That was a high-class performance and he probably ran at least as well in defeat when going on to push Palace Pier all the way to the line in the Prix Jacques le Marois, ultimately going down by a neck.

Poetic Flare also filled the runner-up spot in the Sussex Stakes at Goodwood, a race won by **Alcohol Free** (122) to cement her status as the leading three-year-old filly in this division after a few of them had taken it in turns to beat each other earlier in the season. Alcohol Free also won the Coronation Stakes at Royal Ascot, decisively beating Snow **Lantern** (120) and **Mother Earth** (118), both horses who had her measure on at least one occasion last season. For example, Alcohol Free could manage only fifth when Mother Earth won the 1000 Guineas at Newmarket, while that pair both had to settle for minor honours behind Snow Lantern when she enjoyed her day in the sun in the Falmouth Stakes on the July Course.

The tough Mother Earth made a total of 11 appearances in 2021, all at the top level, and she probably deserved more for her efforts than just two wins, the other coming in the Prix Rothschild at Deauville. She also finished third to **No Speak Alexander** (115) in the Matron Stakes at Leopardstown and second to **Saffron Beach** (119) in the Sun Chariot Stakes at Newmarket. The Irish 1000 Guineas at the Curragh, won by stablemate Empress **Josephine** (114), was one of the few top-level prizes at the trip that Mother Earth missed, while the only time she finished worse than fifth was in the Breeders' Cup Mile at Del Mar. The European contingent still came out on top in California as **Space Blues** (124) brought the curtain down on a fine career with another Group 1 win, his third in total and his second in a row after the Prix de la Foret at Longchamp the previous month.

Middle-distances

St Mark's Basilica (132) could have featured in the previous section given that he began his winning sequence last season in the Poule d'Essai des Poulains at Longchamp, but it was over middle-distances that he really made his name with three further Group 1 wins in the Prix du Jockey Club at Chantilly, the Eclipse at Sandown and the Irish Champion Stakes at Leopardstown. He put up his best display in winning the Eclipse, showing a decisive turn of foot in a tactical race to win by three and a half lengths in ready fashion. Admittedly, the pair who filled the next two places, **Addeybb** (125) and **Mishriff** (131), weren't quite on song returning from absences, but St Mark's Basilica was still full value for a top-class performance, the best by any horse over any distance in 2021.

Mishriff began his four-year-old campaign by winning two hugely valuable prizes in the Middle East, first the Saudi Cup on the dirt at King Abdulaziz Racecourse and then the Dubai Sheema Classic on the turf at Meydan. As versatile as he is talented, Mishriff produced another performance out of the very top drawer when winning the Juddmonte International at York by six lengths—his first Group 1 win on British soil—but not before being put firmly in his place by another top three-year-old in the King George VI & Queen Elizabeth Stakes at Ascot. The horse to beat him there was **Adayar** (131), who became the first Derby winner since Galileo in 2001 to also win the

St Mark's Basilica went unbeaten in four starts in 2021

King George, putting his stamp on the race in the final furlong to beat Mishriff by a length and three quarters, with the same distance back to the Prince of Wales's Stakes winner **Love** (122) in third. Adayar and Mishriff met again in the Champion Stakes back at Ascot later in the season, but neither horse was involved at the finish this time as the Prix du Jockey Club runner-up **Sealiway** (127) and the very progressive **Dubai Honour** (125) fought it out ahead of the Irish 2000 Guineas winner **Mac Swiney** (121). Mishriff and Adayar finished fourth and fifth, respectively, with neither horse at their best for one reason or another.

The ground was put forward as an excuse for Mishriff, while Adayar was possibly feeling the effects of a hard race in the Prix de l'Arc de Triomphe at Longchamp just 13 days earlier. The 14-strong field for the Arc typically featured many of Europe's top middle-distance performers, but the race delivered a huge shock as the German raider **Torquator Tasso** (130) left his previous efforts behind to defy odds of 68/1, staying on best of all in very testing conditions to win by three quarters of a length from **Tarnawa** (125) and **Hurricane Lane** (128), who were split by just a short head in the battle for second. The form had a rock-solid look to it given that the runner-up had made St Mark's Basilica pull out all the stops in the Irish Champion Stakes on her previous appearance, while Hurricane Lane had completed a Group 1 hat-trick since finishing third to stablemate Adayar in the Derby, his wins coming in the Irish Derby at the Curragh, the Grand Prix de Paris at Longchamp and the St Leger at Doncaster. Adayar was back in fourth in the Arc, with Sealiway fifth and **Snowfall** (122) sixth.

Snowfall had looked a potential top-notcher earlier in the year when registering wide-margin wins in the Oaks at Epsom, the Irish Oaks at the Curragh and the Yorkshire Oaks at York. However, she ended the campaign with three successive defeats, finishing second to **Teona** (120) in the Prix Vermeille at Longchamp and third to **Eshaada** (120p) in the Fillies' & Mares' Stakes at Ascot either side of her Arc effort. The pick of the other mares was **Wonderful Tonight** (122), who dished out a comprehensive beating to very smart rivals such as **Broome** (123) and **Hukum** (124) in the Hardwicke Stakes at Royal Ascot. Wonderful Tonight was sadly ruled out of the Arc due to injury, while the Sir Mark Prescott-trained **Alpinista** (121), a three-time Group 1 winner in Germany, would have been another interesting participant at Longchamp, with her defeat of Torquator Tasso in the Grosser Preis von Berlin at Hoppegarten now looking much better than it did at the time.

The French-trained **Skalleti** (124) was another multiple Group 1 winner on the continent, registering victories in the Prix d'Ispahan at Longchamp and the Grosser Dallmayr-Preis at Munich, while Dubai Turf winner **Lord North** (128) and Joseph O'Brien's Cox Plate winner **State of Rest** (123) both enjoyed high-profile triumphs on the international stage. Similar comments apply to **Yibir** (126), who completed a Breeders' Cup hat-trick for Charlie Appleby when winning the Turf, putting him in the same bracket as stablemates Adayar and Hurricane Lane amongst the leading three-year-olds over middle-distances. In Hong Kong, **Pyledriver** (123) had to settle for second in the Vase, but the four-year-old had already given William Muir and Chris Grassick a first Group 1 winner by then, having seen off the quirky **Al Aasy** (122§) in the Coronation Cup at Epsom.

Stayers

Subjectivist (130) ran out a dominant winner of the Gold Cup at Royal Ascot, improving again three months on from his six-length victory in the Dubai Gold Cup at Meydan to complete a relentless rise to the top of the staying ranks. Admittedly, a few of his main rivals at Ascot—including **Stradivarius** (123)—endured traffic problems, but it was still hard not be impressed by the manner in which he settled matters from the home turn, ultimately winning by five lengths from **Princess Zoe** (118). Subjectivist is right up there with the best modern stayers judged on that display and it's just a shame that he was forced to miss the rest of the campaign due to a serious leg injury which will reportedly keep him out of action until 2023.

Stradivarius might have come up short in his bid to win the Gold Cup for a fourth time, but he showed that he still retained plenty of ability at the age of seven with three

Trueshan will continue to take plenty of beating in the staying ranks in 2022

wins in pattern company. Those victories in the Sagaro Stakes at Ascot, the Lonsdale Cup at York and the Doncaster Cup took his career record to 19 wins from 32 starts and he will get the opportunity to add to that tally as he remains in training in 2022. The Gold Cup and the Goodwood Cup will reportedly be his main targets, putting him on a likely collision course again with old rival **Trueshan** (126) who proved to be Stradivarius' nemesis on his final two starts of last season.

In the absence of Stradivarius due to the soft going, Trueshan registered his first Group 1 success in the Goodwood Cup by three and three quarter lengths from **Away He Goes** (118). Incidentally, the multiple Group 2 winner **Sir Ron Priestley** (123)—a half-brother to Subjectivist as well as being his stablemate—suffered a serious injury of his own in finishing third at Goodwood, bringing a premature end to his career. Trueshan, on the other hand, continued to go from strength to strength, putting up a high-class display to win the Prix du Cadran at Longchamp and then repeating his 2020 victory in the Long Distance Cup at Ascot. He'll be a serious contender for top staying honours again in 2022, though his appearances are likely to be dictated again by the ground (yet to race on ground firmer than good).

Stradivarius filled the runner-up spot in the Prix du Cadran, but that position was wrestled from his grasp in the Long Distance Cup by the three-year-old **Tashkhan** (121), who seemed to excel himself up in grade at odds of 50/1. Last year's classic crop threw up several horses who could make an impact in this division in 2022, including **Mojo Star** (122), who still has longer trips to explore after finishing second in both the Derby and the St Leger. **Scope** (121) finished only sixth at Doncaster, but he left that form behind when recording back-to-back wins in a listed race at Ascot and the Prix Royal-Oak at Longchamp. The filly **Free Wind** (119p) won the Park Hill Stakes over the St Leger course and distance by seven lengths, while **Manobo** (119p), who was ineligible to run in the classics as a gelding, created a good impression in going unbeaten in four starts, culminating with a cosy win in the Prix Chaudenay at Longchamp. Manobo made a stylish winning return at Meydan in February, improving his rating to 122p.

Over in Ireland, Ebor winner **Sonnyboyliston** (122) showed very smart form when taking the step up to Group 1 company in his stride in the Irish St Leger at the Curragh, finding plenty to beat **Twilight Payment** (120) by three quarters of a length. **Search For A Song** (120) finished only sixth as she tried to win that race for the third year in a row, but she bounced back to her best with an easy success in the Loughbrown Stakes at the same course two weeks later. Twilight Payment went on to Australia to try and repeat his 2020 triumph in the Melbourne Cup at Flemington, but he ultimately finished well down the field, with the Yorkshire Cup winner **Spanish Mission** (121) faring best of the small European contingent in third.

2021 STATISTICS

TRAINERS (1,2,3 earnings)		Horses	Indiv'l Wnrs	Races Won	Runs	% Strike Rate	Stakes £
1	Charlie Appleby	137	74	116	402	28.9	4,743,539
2	John & Thady Gosden	212	101	133	651	20.4	4,139,911
3	Andrew Balding	209	101	150	922	16.3	4,033,706
4	William Haggas	185	102	174	700	24.9	3,968,304
5	Aidan O'Brien, Ireland	66	9	11	119	9.2	3,006,269
6	Mark Johnston	260	130	212	1,519	14.0	3,002,887
7	Richard Hannon	240	102	146	1,239	11.8	2,827,257
8	Roger Varian	191	98	133	626	21.2	2,500,410
9	Ralph Beckett	140	59	82	514	16.0	1,782,311
10	Tim Easterby	176	77	136	1,349	10.1	1,749,158

JOCKEYS (by winners)		1st	2nd	3rd	Unpl	Total Rides	% Strike Rate
1	Oisin Murphy	183	148	114	416	861	21.3
2	Tom Marquand	176	133	144	615	1068	16.5
3	Hollie Doyle	172	152	153	712	1189	14.5
4	William Buick	170	127	90	416	803	21.2
5	David Probert	170	143	147	776	1236	13.8
6	Richard Kingscote	128	146	138	556	968	13.2
7	Ben Curtis	123	110	103	480	816	15.1
8	Rossa Ryan	120	90	108	462	780	15.4
9	James Doyle	118	130	90	304	642	18.4
10	Jack Mitchell	116	94	97	409	716	16.2

SIRES OF WINNERS (1,2,3 earnings)		Races Won	Runs	% Strike Rate	Stakes £
1	Frankel (by Galileo)	130	679	19.1	4,297,583
2	Dubawi (by Dubai Millennium)	155	719	21.6	3,177,782
3	Sea The Stars (by Cape Cross)	109	546	20.0	3,046,129
4	Dark Angel (by Acclamation)	181	1366	13.3	2,280,995
5	Kingman (by Invincible Spirit)	93	523	17.8	1,931,032
6	Galileo (by Sadler's Wells)	27	300	9.0	1,723,803
7	Lope de Vega (by Shamardal)	112	779	14.4	1,705,660
8	Kodiac (by Danehill)	155	1519	10.2	1,517,387
9	No Nay Never (by Scat Daddy)	54	385	14.0	1,502,421
10	Zoffany (by Dansili)	61	681	9.0	1,279,859

LEADING HORSES (1,2,3 earnings)		Races Won	% Strike Rate	Stakes £
1	Adayar 3 b.c Frankel - Anna Salai	2	40.0	1,168,773
2	Alcohol Free 3 b.f No Nay Never - Plying	3	42.9	857,889
3	Mishriff 4 b.c Make Believe - Contradict	1	25.0	819,785
4	Baaeed 3 b.c Sea The Stars - Aghareed	5	100.0	720,458
5	Sealiway 3 ch.c Galiway - Kensea	1	100.0	714,546
6	Palace Pier 4 b.c Kingman - Beach Frolic	3	75.0	702,831
7	Hurricane Lane 3 ch.c Frankel - Gale Force	3	75.0	644,347
8	Poetic Flare 3 b.c Dawn Approach - Maria Lee	2	66.7	640,504
9	Lady Bowthorpe 5 b.f Nathaniel - Maglietta Fina	2	33.3	616,255
10	Love 4 ch.f Galileo - Pikaboo	1	33.3	598,720

SECTION 5

THE TIMEFORM TOP 100

2 Year Olds

Rating	Horse
122p	Native Trail
118p	Luxembourg
116p	Coroebus
115p	Tenebrism
115	Modern Games
114p	Point Lonsdale
114	Angel Bleu
114	Dubawi Legend
114	Perfect Power
113	Bayside Boy
113	Ebro River
113	Reach For The Moon
112p	Atomic Force
112p	Inspiral
112	Castle Star
112	Lusail
112	Noble Truth
111	Armor
111	El Bodegon
111	Flotus
111	Go Bears Go
111	Hannibal Barca
111	Sissoko
110p	Aikhal
110	Caturra
110	Dr Zempf
110	Flaming Rib
110	Royal Patronage
110	Sacred Bridge
110	Twilight Jet
109p	Light Infantry
109	Imperial Fighter
108p	Jumbly
108p	King of Bavaria
108p	Stone Age
108p	Trident
108	Asymmetric
107p	Discoveries
107p	Triple Time
107	Berkshire Shadow
107	Straight Answer
107	Twilight Gleaming
106	Agartha
106	Masekela
106	Quick Suzy
105p	Buckaroo
105p	Goldspur
105p	Hoo Ya Mal
105p	Tatsumaki
105	Hello You
105	Hierarchy
105	Sandrine
105	The Wizard of Eye
105	Wings of War
105	Zain Claudette
104p	Hafit
104	Cachet
104	Cresta
104	Gis A Sub
104	Gisburn
104	Gubbass
104	Have A Good Day
104	Prosperous Voyage
104	Unconquerable
104	Witch Hunter
104	Zechariah
103p	New Science
103p	Tacarib Bay
103	Albahr
103	Dillian
103	Fearby
103	Great Max
103	Mise En Scene
102p	El Caballo
102	Canonized
102	Chipotle
102	Desert Dreamer
102	Glounthaune
102	Gwan So
102	Harrow
102	Honey Sweet
102	Kaufymaker
102	Khunan
102	Korker
102	Last Crusader
102	Masseto
102	Nazanin
102	Oneforthegutter
102	Sam Maximus
102	Vertiginous
102	Wild Beauty
101p	Westover
101	Alflaila
101	Corazon
101	Dhabab
101	Dubai Poet
101	Ehraz
101	Fast Attack
101	Geocentric
101	Hellomydarlin
101	Mr Professor
101	Papa Don't Preach
101	Power of Beauty
101	Tezzaray

3 Year Olds

Rating	Horse
133p	Flightline
132	St Mark's Basilica
131	Adayar
130	Baaeed
129	Life Is Good
128	Hurricane Lane
128	Jackie's Warrior
127	Efforia
127	Poetic Flare
127	Sealiway
126	Dr. Schivel
126	Golden Pal
126	Medina Spirit
126	Yibir
125	Dubai Honour
125	Essential Quality
125	Home Affairs
125	Pixie Knight
125	Suesa
124	Aldaary
123	Creative Force
123	Mendocino
123	State of Rest
123	Winter Power
122	Alcohol Free
122	Dragon Symbol
122	Master of The Seas
122	Mojo Star
122	Snowfall
121	A Case of You
121	Lone Eagle
121	Lucky Vega
121	Mac Swiney
121	Rohaan
121	Scope
121	Sisfahan
121	Tashkhan
120p	Eshaada
120	Bolshoi Ballet
120	Bubble Gift
120	Foxes Tales
120	Masen
120	Mostahdaf
120	Siskany
120	Snow Lantern
120	Teona
119p	Free Wind
119	Rougir
119	Saffron Beach
119	Santa Barbara
118p	Bay Bridge
118	Alenquer
118	Logo Hunter
118	Loving Dream
118	Megallan
118	Millebosc
118	Mother Earth
118	Power Under Me
118	Rebel's Romance
118	The Highway Rat
118	The Mediterranean
118	Title
117	Campanelle
117	Create Belief
117	El Drama
117	Minzaal
117	Mohaafeth

116p Manobo
116 Derab
116 Earlswood
116 Jumby
116 Modern News
116 Novemba
116 Qaader
115p Storm Damage
115 Battleground
115 Cadillac
115 Chindit
115 Happy Romance
115 Highland Avenue
115 King of The Castle
115 La Petite Coco
115 Laneqash
115 Laws of Indices
115 No Speak Alexander
115 Palmas
115 Primo Bacio
115 Sacred
115 Saiydabad
115 Tasman Bay
115 Thunder Moon
114 Coeursamba
114 Empress Josephine
114 Fancy Man
114 Interpretation
114 Joan of Arc
114 Maximal
114 Naval Crown
114 Perotto
114 Spycatcher
114 Vadream

Older Horses

131 Mishriff
130 Knicks Go
130 Subjectivist
130 Torquator Tasso
129 Charlatan
129 Golden Sixty
129 Incentivise
129 Nature Strip
129 Palace Pier
128 Gamine
127 Mystic Guide
127 Verry Elleegant
126 Contrail
126 Deep Bond
126 Eduardo
126 More Than This
126 Trueshan
126 Waikuku
126 Zaaki
125 Addeybb
125 Glory Vase
125 Gran Alegria
125 Letruska
125 Lord North
125 Masked Crusader
125 Monomoy Girl
125 Southern Legend
125 Starman
125 T O Keynes
125 Tarnawa
125 Zenden
124 Chrono Genesis
124 Hukum
124 Skalleti
124 Space Blues
123 Broome
123 Dream of Dreams
123 Loves Only You
123 Motakhayyel
123 Pyledriver
123 Sir Ron Priestley
122 Armory
122 Helvic Dream
122 Khuzaam
122 Lord Glitters
122 Love
122 Marianafoot
122 Secret Ambition
122 Sky Field
122 Sonnyboyliston
122 Wonderful Tonight
122§ Al Aasy
121 Alpinista
121 Art Power
121 Baron Samedi
121 Oxted
121 Spanish Mission
121 Stradivarius
121 The Revenant
121 Walton Street
120p Real World
120 Audarya
120 Benbatl
120 Emaraaty Ana
120 Grand Glory
120 In Swoop
120 Iresine
120 Lady Bowthorpe
120 Lope Y Fernandez
120 Military Law
120 Order of Australia
120 Salute The Soldier
120 Search For A Song
120 Twilight Payment
120 Victor Ludorum
119 Al Suhail
119 Albaflora
119 Duhail
119 Ebaiyra
119 Glen Shiel
119 Glorious Journey
119 Good Effort
119 Gustavus Weston
119 Kinross
119 Lancaster House
119 Lazuli
119 Nahaarr
119 Nerium
119 Speak of The Devil
119 Tilsit
118 Away He Goes
118 Barney Roy
118 Berneuil
118 Canvassed
118 Cape Byron
118 Danyah
118 Dubai Future
118 Ecrivain
118 Emperor of The Sun
118 Equilateral
118 Global Giant
118 Japan
118 Kaspar
118 Magny Cours
118 Maker of Kings
118 My Oberon
118 Passion And Glory
118 Pogo
118 Princess Zoe
118 Sir Busker
118 Solid Stone
118 Tabera
118 Tis Marvellous
118 Top Rank
118 Wally

TRAINERS FOR COURSES

The following statistics show the most successful trainers over the past five seasons at each of the courses that stage Flat racing in England, Scotland and Wales. Impact Value is expressed as a factor of a trainer's number of winners compared to those expected to occur by chance. Market Value is expressed as the factor by which the % chance of an Industry Starting Price exceeds random, as implied by field size. For example, a horse that is shorter than 3/1 in a 4-runner field will have a market value above 1.

ASCOT

Trainer	Wins	Runs	Strike Rate	% Rivals Beaten	P/L	Run To Form %	Impact Value	Market Value
John Gosden	41	241	17.01%	57.31	-43.10	45.44	1.87	1.96
William Haggas	29	198	14.65%	58.44	-47.48	40.02	1.58	1.79
Charlie Appleby	27	154	17.53%	61.54	-19.80	52.35	1.94	2.01
Roger Varian	26	193	13.47%	56.69	-47.97	43.56	1.58	1.60
Aidan O'Brien, Ireland	26	272	9.56%	52.63	-134.83	46.69	1.09	1.71
Andrew Balding	25	258	9.69%	51.98	-84.30	43.98	1.01	1.19
Mark Johnston	21	245	8.57%	47.85	-117.88	38.78	0.97	1.16
Clive Cox	19	143	13.29%	55.41	136.35	45.77	1.50	1.38
Richard Hannon	18	288	6.25%	45.33	-53.56	30.67	0.70	0.98
Sir Michael Stoute	17	136	12.50%	61.31	-38.68	54.13	1.26	1.81

AYR

Trainer	Wins	Runs	Strike Rate	% Rivals Beaten	P/L	Run To Form %	Impact Value	Market Value
Keith Dalgleish	48	522	9.20%	51.14	-147.40	35.83	0.82	1.05
Jim Goldie	47	518	9.07%	48.62	-103.17	33.14	0.82	0.97
Richard Fahey	34	324	10.49%	53.12	-113.90	37.26	0.98	1.25
David O'Meara	31	218	14.22%	55.36	-32.04	41.54	1.24	1.49
R. Mike Smith	29	229	12.66%	47.03	52.13	32.11	1.17	0.93
Iain Jardine	28	276	10.14%	45.97	-51.63	29.78	0.91	1.00
Michael Dods	28	255	10.98%	52.65	-49.54	38.77	1.03	1.42
Tim Easterby	25	200	12.50%	57.48	45.09	39.06	1.36	1.51
Mark Johnston	25	177	14.12%	49.31	-79.09	35.00	1.05	1.42
Kevin Ryan	20	176	11.36%	49.59	-59.51	34.05	1.12	1.31

BATH

Trainer	Wins	Runs	Strike Rate	% Rivals Beaten	P/L	Run To Form %	Impact Value	Market Value
Tony Carroll	31	247	12.55%	49.87	-51.95	30.77	1.15	1.06
Clive Cox	27	111	24.32%	63.96	25.86	44.71	1.93	1.95
Mark Johnston	27	110	24.55%	59.98	0.40	49.48	1.54	1.57
Ronald Harris	24	186	12.90%	51.29	-8.71	34.48	1.07	1.04
Richard Hannon	23	157	14.65%	53.20	-62.11	34.72	1.10	1.47
Malcolm Saunders	19	135	14.07%	49.32	-31.47	34.32	1.15	1.12
Mick Channon	19	116	16.38%	54.37	-20.63	37.40	1.37	1.38
Rod Millman	17	137	12.41%	49.34	10.13	36.81	1.04	1.15
Charles Hills	15	77	19.48%	51.57	-24.26	40.77	1.29	1.44
Adrian Wintle	15	57	26.32%	66.24	58.13	50.88	2.60	1.37

BEVERLEY

Trainer	Wins	Runs	Strike Rate	% Rivals Beaten	P/L	Run To Form %	Impact Value	Market Value
Tim Easterby	50	448	11.16%	50.25	-136.55	34.26	1.05	1.20
Mark Johnston	49	231	21.21%	57.30	-40.07	48.85	1.60	1.76
Richard Fahey	47	365	12.88%	54.77	-104.99	41.21	1.14	1.37
David O'Meara	39	254	15.35%	57.29	-5.19	40.24	1.32	1.42
Kevin Ryan	26	156	16.67%	59.43	-36.36	44.98	1.51	1.59
Nigel Tinkler	26	203	12.81%	49.84	44.33	34.09	1.27	1.02
Roger Fell	14	155	9.03%	47.63	-56.46	24.83	0.85	1.13
Michael Dods	14	123	11.38%	51.14	-29.25	32.67	1.08	1.37
Karen Tutty	13	79	16.46%	59.22	32.75	38.47	1.73	1.22
Bryan Smart	13	119	10.92%	54.78	-41.17	37.64	1.04	1.16

BRIGHTON

Trainer	Wins	Runs	Strike Rate	% Rivals Beaten	P/L	Run To Form %	Impact Value	Market Value
Tony Carroll	40	315	12.70%	51.82	-100.34	36.46	0.99	1.20
Richard Hannon	31	127	24.41%	61.96	50.92	52.88	1.72	1.50
Gary Moore	27	177	15.25%	53.94	24.58	36.12	1.25	1.33
Eve Johnson Houghton	19	105	18.10%	55.86	-4.90	39.83	1.34	1.47
Richard Hughes	18	78	23.08%	58.38	3.27	45.37	1.54	1.42
Mark Johnston	18	102	17.65%	50.60	-37.15	33.13	1.18	1.50
John Gallagher	16	98	16.33%	49.57	8.20	33.92	1.23	1.12
Andrew Balding	13	58	22.41%	58.09	-8.90	46.55	1.35	1.52
Archie Watson	12	50	24.00%	58.46	-5.13	36.75	1.43	1.60
Stuart Williams	12	61	19.67%	57.10	-3.93	45.90	1.40	1.48

CARLISLE

Trainer	Wins	Runs	Strike Rate	% Rivals Beaten	P/L	Run To Form %	Impact Value	Market Value
Keith Dalgleish	27	194	13.92%	50.96	-3.50	30.94	1.21	1.18
Richard Fahey	25	189	13.23%	54.00	-12.46	35.77	1.15	1.25
Tim Easterby	24	273	8.79%	50.73	-82.29	32.76	0.81	1.19
Mark Johnston	20	95	21.05%	64.14	18.21	54.57	1.57	1.41
K. R. Burke	17	100	17.00%	58.02	-1.28	46.23	1.41	1.53
Kevin Ryan	15	89	16.85%	59.84	-24.53	40.45	1.47	1.49
Michael Dods	15	133	11.28%	53.63	-52.30	37.88	1.01	1.36
Roger Fell	11	78	14.10%	55.57	-7.50	37.84	1.33	1.19
Dianne Sayer	11	67	16.42%	52.77	0.07	45.16	1.47	1.40
Nigel Tinkler	10	40	25.00%	59.08	33.50	52.94	2.45	1.34

CATTERICK BRIDGE

Trainer	Wins	Runs	Strike Rate	% Rivals Beaten	P/L	Run To Form %	Impact Value	Market Value
Tim Easterby	41	337	12.17%	54.80	-31.86	34.82	1.12	1.12
Richard Fahey	28	212	13.21%	55.42	-59.37	36.05	1.12	1.30
David O'Meara	27	189	14.29%	54.17	-98.22	30.05	1.24	1.61
Keith Dalgleish	22	129	17.05%	53.91	66.83	38.21	1.46	1.25
Mark Johnston	22	134	16.42%	51.39	-33.54	42.15	1.24	1.43
John Quinn	18	172	10.47%	49.81	-62.45	29.36	0.97	1.31
Ruth Carr	15	152	9.87%	53.03	-9.25	29.14	1.01	1.22
Michael Dods	15	88	17.05%	58.05	45.08	44.13	1.58	1.56
K. R. Burke	14	73	19.18%	52.88	30.55	43.84	1.56	1.35
Kevin Ryan	14	73	19.18%	59.45	11.81	46.47	1.77	1.58

CHELMSFORD CITY (AW)

Trainer	Wins	Runs	Strike Rate	% Rivals Beaten	P/L	Run To Form %	Impact Value	Market Value
Mark Johnston	82	497	16.50%	54.70	-63.93	47.82	1.22	1.34
Michael Appleby	71	610	11.64%	50.58	-106.44	34.38	1.01	1.16
John Gosden	59	239	24.69%	67.77	-42.17	57.89	1.93	2.27
Stuart Williams	51	395	12.91%	56.72	-140.90	40.80	1.12	1.40
David Simcock	50	298	16.78%	53.84	-41.21	40.27	1.23	1.15
Saeed bin Suroor	46	185	24.86%	64.16	-38.08	55.77	2.03	2.23
William Haggas	46	197	23.35%	66.72	-40.20	52.15	1.88	2.35
Richard Hughes	44	219	20.09%	62.15	36.68	54.55	1.75	1.46
Sir Michael Stoute	37	151	24.50%	61.62	-31.73	54.99	1.97	2.11
Dean Ivory	35	321	10.90%	51.35	-60.90	32.18	1.02	1.13

CHEPSTOW

Trainer	Wins	Runs	Strike Rate	% Rivals Beaten	P/L	Run To Form %	Impact Value	Market Value
David Evans	26	221	11.76%	50.55	-34.02	36.69	1.03	1.09
Tony Carroll	17	137	12.41%	50.35	-6.00	36.72	1.19	1.10
Ralph Beckett	17	55	30.91%	62.47	16.27	46.22	2.38	1.87
Eve Johnson Houghton	17	77	22.08%	63.27	1.07	44.03	1.75	1.62
Mick Channon	16	104	15.38%	53.84	12.83	43.67	1.34	1.49
John O'Shea	16	133	12.03%	45.14	-2.55	26.19	1.02	0.91
Andrew Balding	14	72	19.44%	59.75	-14.54	46.91	1.56	1.92
Rod Millman	14	102	13.73%	57.33	-35.54	35.66	1.14	1.29
Richard Hannon	14	131	10.69%	52.08	-46.63	37.18	0.88	1.43
Grace Harris	11	115	9.57%	39.18	45.00	19.80	0.92	0.68

CHESTER

Trainer	Wins	Runs	Strike Rate	% Rivals Beaten	P/L	Run To Form %	Impact Value	Market Value
Richard Fahey	53	450	11.78%	55.31	-70.92	35.48	1.04	1.31
Tom Dascombe	43	298	14.43%	51.46	-85.37	39.73	1.15	1.22
Andrew Balding	40	189	21.16%	59.76	28.37	52.68	1.63	1.68
Mark Johnston	31	203	15.27%	55.69	-32.69	46.81	1.20	1.49
Tim Easterby	22	158	13.92%	51.39	-5.00	39.87	1.24	1.13
Ralph Beckett	17	73	23.29%	59.13	-10.43	52.05	1.83	1.58
Ian Williams	16	172	9.30%	48.94	-68.00	34.30	0.84	1.12
William Haggas	13	37	35.14%	68.25	0.20	67.57	2.40	2.43
Richard Hannon	12	70	17.14%	59.94	-23.24	45.71	1.34	1.59
Aidan O'Brien, Ireland	10	31	32.26%	68.97	0.60	73.33	2.33	1.77

DONCASTER

Trainer	Wins	Runs	Strike Rate	% Rivals Beaten	P/L	Run To Form %	Impact Value	Market Value
Roger Varian	40	173	23.12%	67.54	-30.03	56.58	1.99	2.26
Richard Hannon	35	303	11.55%	53.40	-57.36	44.32	1.02	1.29
Richard Fahey	27	359	7.52%	50.11	-133.05	31.25	0.76	1.13
William Haggas	26	119	21.85%	66.40	17.71	54.20	1.94	2.11
Mark Johnston	23	172	13.37%	49.92	-35.27	44.58	1.01	1.16
Sir Michael Stoute	20	77	25.97%	66.18	-5.78	57.63	1.99	2.20
Ralph Beckett	19	101	18.81%	59.44	44.83	53.72	1.68	1.75
John Gosden	18	97	18.56%	62.32	-32.01	51.06	1.60	2.32
Saeed bin Suroor	18	60	30.00%	64.21	18.54	54.48	2.33	2.17
Charlie Appleby	17	75	22.67%	63.76	-17.20	54.23	1.83	2.75

EPSOM

Trainer	Wins	Runs	Strike Rate	% Rivals Beaten	P/L	Run To Form %	Impact Value	Market Value
Mark Johnston	17	110	15.45%	52.75	-20.07	41.82	1.15	1.33
Jim Boyle	13	95	13.68%	46.17	-14.75	36.84	1.09	0.94
Andrew Balding	13	85	15.29%	58.64	-19.08	48.82	1.24	1.72
Ralph Beckett	10	53	18.87%	54.23	-12.92	44.34	1.40	1.29
Charlie Appleby	10	29	34.48%	71.60	38.67	65.52	2.56	1.69
Eve Johnson Houghton	10	40	25.00%	60.68	7.80	48.75	2.02	1.25
Hughie Morrison	9	33	27.27%	61.18	19.55	48.48	2.27	1.37
Gary Moore	9	61	14.75%	52.53	37.75	38.90	1.19	1.13
David O'Meara	9	59	15.25%	55.94	-2.00	38.98	1.35	1.18
Aidan O'Brien, Ireland	8	58	13.79%	56.36	41.35	55.17	1.49	1.39

FFOS LAS

Trainer	Wins	Runs	Strike Rate	% Rivals Beaten	P/L	Run To Form %	Impact Value	Market Value
Andrew Balding	13	46	28.26%	68.45	1.99	64.67	2.07	1.98
Rod Millman	10	58	17.24%	50.71	-14.79	39.66	1.26	1.12
Archie Watson	10	32	31.25%	61.73	8.50	50.00	2.34	1.74
Ed Walker	7	35	20.00%	64.67	12.10	51.17	1.48	1.25
Roger Charlton	7	31	22.58%	63.27	28.69	43.66	1.85	2.08
David Evans	7	110	6.36%	41.10	-61.50	29.64	0.48	0.82
Hughie Morrison	7	25	28.00%	61.00	8.60	44.00	2.24	1.47
Richard Hughes	6	35	17.14%	60.10	3.62	51.43	1.40	1.49
Richard Hannon	5	53	9.43%	57.79	-27.25	36.67	0.75	1.62
Jamie Osborne	5	21	23.81%	72.28	14.50	80.27	1.90	1.48

GOODWOOD

Trainer	Wins	Runs	Strike Rate	% Rivals Beaten	P/L	Run To Form %	Impact Value	Market Value
Mark Johnston	44	316	13.92%	51.62	-70.66	39.92	1.28	1.34
Andrew Balding	33	217	15.21%	56.28	-42.79	52.81	1.31	1.31
William Haggas	28	136	20.59%	59.19	1.01	53.34	1.77	1.82
Richard Hannon	21	283	7.42%	47.15	-102.83	33.49	0.70	1.08
Ralph Beckett	19	119	15.97%	54.84	11.56	44.98	1.39	1.38
John Gosden	19	92	20.65%	58.04	-21.67	51.54	1.63	1.89
Charles Hills	18	129	13.95%	52.16	-21.80	38.52	1.27	1.32
Charlie Appleby	16	73	21.92%	59.99	-18.31	46.58	1.96	2.07
Mick Channon	14	168	8.33%	46.24	-69.17	30.23	0.75	1.00
Sir Michael Stoute	13	83	15.66%	57.84	-41.26	51.81	1.21	1.89

HAMILTON

Trainer	Wins	Runs	Strike Rate	% Rivals Beaten	P/L	Run To Form %	Impact Value	Market Value
Keith Dalgleish	57	434	13.13%	50.39	-28.40	36.62	1.01	1.10
Richard Fahey	38	248	15.32%	53.07	-71.13	41.21	1.13	1.23
Mark Johnston	36	207	17.39%	55.10	-46.02	43.66	1.24	1.52
Tim Easterby	32	175	18.29%	60.47	-11.53	41.38	1.58	1.56
Kevin Ryan	30	134	22.39%	58.77	-14.22	50.73	1.68	1.47
David O'Meara	29	147	19.73%	58.89	-17.27	41.81	1.46	1.54
Iain Jardine	19	221	8.60%	48.77	-88.45	30.70	0.71	1.00
Jim Goldie	17	185	9.19%	47.00	-78.53	31.55	0.81	0.99
Michael Dods	11	84	13.10%	60.44	-16.21	45.11	1.10	1.52
Roger Fell	11	78	14.10%	52.65	-35.67	30.77	1.34	1.49

HAYDOCK PARK

Trainer	Wins	Runs	Strike Rate	% Rivals Beaten	P/L	Run To Form %	Impact Value	Market Value
Tom Dascombe	58	375	15.47%	53.26	100.32	41.23	1.26	1.27
William Haggas	38	164	23.17%	64.20	-37.01	57.03	1.73	2.01
Mark Johnston	38	255	14.90%	53.41	-44.27	42.73	1.10	1.19
Ed Walker	27	116	23.28%	58.37	28.31	49.64	1.87	1.51
Richard Hannon	26	183	14.21%	53.69	-36.79	42.52	1.15	1.21
David O'Meara	22	214	10.28%	50.05	0.08	32.60	0.83	1.09
Kevin Ryan	19	155	12.26%	51.87	-26.00	32.08	1.02	1.14
Richard Fahey	19	289	6.57%	49.02	-142.39	36.95	0.58	0.92
Tim Easterby	19	289	6.57%	47.67	-86.45	28.55	0.61	0.92
Michael Dods	19	103	18.45%	53.82	24.76	37.14	1.64	1.32

KEMPTON PARK (AW)

Trainer	Wins	Runs	Strike Rate	% Rivals Beaten	P/L	Run To Form %	Impact Value	Market Value
John Gosden	76	302	25.17%	68.21	-32.34	56.47	2.40	2.56
Richard Hannon	65	641	10.14%	52.36	-179.31	38.35	0.99	1.25
Roger Varian	64	282	22.70%	69.42	-9.77	55.71	2.30	2.39
Andrew Balding	62	404	15.35%	58.91	49.67	46.88	1.46	1.44
Archie Watson	53	266	19.92%	58.37	-34.78	43.07	1.80	1.71
Roger Charlton	51	278	18.35%	58.14	15.55	46.33	1.81	1.57
Mark Johnston	49	350	14.00%	51.83	-34.60	37.68	1.23	1.30
Charlie Appleby	48	134	35.82%	76.52	-17.01	69.50	3.24	3.70
Ralph Beckett	46	288	15.97%	58.96	3.70	46.41	1.54	1.68
Ed Walker	44	298	14.77%	61.82	-86.26	50.73	1.52	1.67

LEICESTER

Trainer	Wins	Runs	Strike Rate	% Rivals Beaten	P/L	Run To Form %	Impact Value	Market Value
Mark Johnston	25	126	19.84%	53.44	-13.05	43.40	1.36	1.30
Richard Fahey	23	147	15.65%	55.54	-26.99	42.30	1.35	1.41
Richard Hannon	21	167	12.57%	50.01	-55.19	33.25	1.02	1.26
Sir Michael Stoute	17	62	27.42%	67.16	-1.24	67.79	2.01	1.87
Clive Cox	17	112	15.18%	57.19	-9.27	49.61	1.28	1.37
Roger Varian	16	67	23.88%	63.65	-9.84	54.61	1.86	2.15
David Evans	15	102	14.71%	55.18	-23.34	35.00	1.30	1.24
Michael Appleby	14	135	10.37%	46.19	94.08	30.37	0.89	0.96
William Haggas	13	54	24.07%	57.68	-9.19	47.11	1.97	2.00
Michael Bell	12	65	18.46%	51.30	0.50	37.31	1.47	1.08

LINGFIELD PARK (AW)

Trainer	Wins	Runs	Strike Rate	% Rivals Beaten	P/L	Run To Form %	Impact Value	Market Value
Mark Johnston	73	357	20.45%	54.74	10.61	50.85	1.52	1.42
Archie Watson	65	307	21.17%	61.55	-17.08	48.60	1.75	1.70
Richard Hannon	64	408	15.69%	56.49	-23.83	47.18	1.32	1.43
John Gosden	52	193	26.94%	73.95	-4.77	65.68	2.18	2.60
Gary Moore	38	311	12.22%	51.13	-46.68	33.23	1.19	1.22
Simon Dow	35	329	10.64%	50.35	-57.80	37.79	0.96	1.17
Tony Carroll	34	329	10.33%	49.67	-67.63	31.68	0.94	1.12
Andrew Balding	33	219	15.07%	52.92	-4.88	43.40	1.21	1.38
Roger Varian	32	114	28.07%	63.94	15.16	63.92	2.45	2.34
David Evans	31	309	10.03%	49.88	-105.20	33.31	0.85	1.17

LINGFIELD PARK (TURF)

Trainer	Wins	Runs	Strike Rate	% Rivals Beaten	P/L	Run To Form %	Impact Value	Market Value
Richard Hannon	25	141	17.73%	59.58	-9.23	39.05	1.44	1.60
William Haggas	23	57	40.35%	70.88	29.21	60.79	2.93	2.35
Gary Moore	15	109	13.76%	51.36	5.38	30.73	1.13	1.07
John Bridger	14	130	10.77%	48.78	25.58	28.85	1.01	0.88
Mick Channon	13	105	12.38%	56.10	-56.79	43.68	1.00	1.30
Archie Watson	11	55	20.00%	60.63	23.10	50.52	1.43	1.52
Jim Boyle	10	74	13.51%	50.53	3.38	36.80	1.17	1.07
Roger Varian	10	36	27.78%	76.94	8.80	68.31	2.14	2.26
Andrew Balding	9	50	18.00%	52.77	-7.36	37.24	1.28	1.75
Mark Johnston	9	57	15.79%	47.54	-28.92	31.74	1.05	1.48

MUSSELBURGH

Trainer	Wins	Runs	Strike Rate	% Rivals Beaten	P/L	Run To Form %	Impact Value	Market Value
Keith Dalgleish	60	480	12.50%	51.22	-107.20	34.55	1.01	1.14
Richard Fahey	42	223	18.83%	56.56	46.39	46.40	1.46	1.28
Iain Jardine	35	241	14.52%	49.60	1.74	39.34	1.16	1.11
Mark Johnston	35	197	17.77%	56.39	-5.63	47.17	1.26	1.51
Tim Easterby	22	228	9.65%	49.79	-67.55	32.16	0.82	1.30
Jim Goldie	21	247	8.50%	49.41	-82.75	30.21	0.75	0.96
Rebecca Bastiman	19	135	14.07%	62.65	-1.75	38.82	1.29	1.17
David O'Meara	14	112	12.50%	53.83	-35.43	35.71	0.99	1.50
Paul Midgley	14	131	10.69%	47.67	-14.09	27.48	0.95	1.23
Archie Watson	11	24	45.83%	66.82	23.19	54.17	3.51	2.06

NEWBURY

Trainer	Wins	Runs	Strike Rate	% Rivals Beaten	P/L	Run To Form %	Impact Value	Market Value
Richard Hannon	57	464	12.28%	55.36	-23.86	43.08	1.25	1.22
William Haggas	41	197	20.81%	60.84	-3.53	46.99	2.01	2.14
John Gosden	37	139	26.62%	70.59	17.05	67.45	2.53	2.76
Roger Charlton	28	162	17.28%	53.83	38.12	43.04	1.74	1.41
Andrew Balding	24	228	10.53%	56.02	67.59	45.94	1.00	1.31
Roger Varian	22	146	15.07%	61.47	-6.03	49.49	1.56	1.88
Ed Walker	19	152	12.50%	57.59	-34.68	44.20	1.31	1.37
Charlie Appleby	17	59	28.81%	66.53	3.63	52.61	2.28	2.36
Sir Michael Stoute	14	93	15.05%	62.57	-33.42	43.05	1.39	1.81
Charles Hills	13	173	7.51%	50.95	-50.75	34.97	0.76	1.09

NEWCASTLE (AW)

Trainer	Wins	Runs	Strike Rate	% Rivals Beaten	P/L	Run To Form %	Impact Value	Market Value
Richard Fahey	91	755	12.05%	54.60	-70.39	38.45	1.13	1.19
Jim Goldie	54	461	11.71%	54.63	76.37	30.69	1.18	1.19
Mark Johnston	48	446	10.76%	50.66	-103.17	37.14	0.90	1.30
John Gosden	47	145	32.41%	74.08	-16.71	64.58	2.59	3.03
Keith Dalgleish	45	409	11.00%	49.83	-93.23	37.35	1.04	1.21
K. R. Burke	43	372	11.56%	53.57	78.32	37.00	1.04	1.20
Antony Brittain	39	413	9.44%	52.48	-93.45	31.93	0.98	1.15
Roger Varian	39	163	23.93%	72.30	-40.74	61.23	2.21	2.79
Ben Haslam	39	311	12.54%	51.37	28.46	36.48	1.23	1.19
William Haggas	38	128	29.69%	72.21	2.56	62.28	2.46	2.51

NEWMARKET (JULY)

Trainer	Wins	Runs	Strike Rate	% Rivals Beaten	P/L	Run To Form %	Impact Value	Market Value
Charlie Appleby	55	195	28.21%	69.49	-9.29	61.54	2.20	2.36
Richard Hannon	46	328	14.02%	53.83	-20.62	43.04	1.15	1.17
Mark Johnston	38	213	17.84%	52.04	-12.34	47.42	1.34	1.27
John Gosden	37	175	21.14%	57.86	-8.26	45.75	1.67	1.83
William Haggas	23	143	16.08%	56.57	-55.34	39.58	1.29	1.60
Saeed bin Suroor	22	74	29.73%	67.29	19.91	58.29	2.29	1.85
Andrew Balding	20	117	17.09%	56.96	3.33	48.95	1.40	1.28
Roger Varian	16	130	12.31%	54.90	-38.75	44.51	1.00	1.57
Hugo Palmer	14	119	11.76%	48.14	-34.63	42.08	0.89	1.11
Sir Michael Stoute	13	96	13.54%	48.38	-42.25	31.97	1.02	1.37

NEWMARKET (ROWLEY)

Trainer	Wins	Runs	Strike Rate	% Rivals Beaten	P/L	Run To Form %	Impact Value	Market Value
Charlie Appleby	76	262	29.01%	67.97	38.21	62.16	2.36	2.19
John Gosden	53	270	19.63%	62.45	5.80	50.47	1.75	1.92
Roger Varian	35	236	14.83%	59.61	-18.74	48.35	1.42	1.61
Mark Johnston	35	274	12.77%	49.69	-40.35	40.00	1.05	1.14
William Haggas	32	239	13.39%	52.01	-27.08	38.68	1.29	1.48
Andrew Balding	30	236	12.71%	56.83	21.35	46.88	1.16	1.32
Aidan O'Brien, Ireland	27	172	15.70%	58.05	-2.35	53.49	1.50	1.77
Ralph Beckett	25	154	16.23%	56.94	20.56	52.38	1.51	1.54
Richard Hannon	25	361	6.93%	49.11	-64.50	38.66	0.64	1.01
Saeed bin Suroor	14	101	13.86%	61.01	17.38	47.47	1.35	1.81

NOTTINGHAM

Trainer	Wins	Runs	Strike Rate	% Rivals Beaten	P/L	Run To Form %	Impact Value	Market Value
Michael Appleby	42	254	16.54%	49.46	85.23	35.37	1.48	1.15
Richard Hannon	23	162	14.20%	53.47	-7.88	39.12	1.22	1.19
Richard Fahey	21	178	11.80%	53.00	-38.42	42.99	0.99	1.15
Mark Johnston	21	150	14.00%	52.06	-66.74	41.70	1.03	1.31
Roger Varian	20	100	20.00%	64.27	-10.13	50.80	1.85	2.25
William Haggas	19	71	26.76%	68.16	6.64	51.01	2.60	2.37
Sir Michael Stoute	16	60	26.67%	63.01	23.13	54.14	2.22	1.76
Ian Williams	16	76	21.05%	53.12	32.04	42.70	1.92	1.21
Mick Channon	16	97	16.49%	55.27	68.19	46.31	1.47	1.27
K. R. Burke	15	104	14.42%	57.09	-3.01	44.75	1.19	1.30

PONTEFRACT

Trainer	Wins	Runs	Strike Rate	% Rivals Beaten	P/L	Run To Form %	Impact Value	Market Value
Richard Fahey	41	315	13.02%	55.86	-24.46	37.96	1.10	1.26
Tim Easterby	34	282	12.06%	50.04	-88.63	32.07	1.01	1.10
Mark Johnston	34	210	16.19%	50.29	-61.74	39.87	1.10	1.40
David O'Meara	29	178	16.29%	55.08	-16.60	37.67	1.34	1.24
Paul Midgley	20	132	15.15%	52.22	29.33	25.76	1.39	1.23
Kevin Ryan	20	123	16.26%	54.00	-8.60	41.32	1.31	1.30
Richard Whitaker	16	63	25.40%	59.83	38.08	39.68	2.49	1.35
Sir Michael Stoute	15	46	32.61%	67.30	10.63	53.22	2.06	2.56
Micky Hammond	14	121	11.57%	48.66	-26.25	31.65	1.03	0.91
K. R. Burke	13	89	14.61%	54.26	-31.07	45.51	1.20	1.29

REDCAR

Trainer	Wins	Runs	Strike Rate	% Rivals Beaten	P/L	Run To Form %	Impact Value	Market Value
Tim Easterby	45	521	8.64%	49.69	-96.40	30.64	0.91	1.11
Richard Fahey	35	311	11.25%	56.04	-63.13	36.98	1.18	1.42
David O'Meara	35	255	13.73%	55.41	20.90	35.35	1.35	1.41
Michael Dods	20	225	8.89%	51.73	-37.22	33.83	0.94	1.27
William Haggas	19	54	35.19%	72.06	2.93	61.77	3.13	2.92
Mark Johnston	19	134	14.18%	48.90	-51.24	37.15	1.21	1.47
David Barron	16	130	12.31%	58.09	-22.55	37.88	1.33	1.34
Declan Carroll	16	93	17.20%	54.26	61.25	29.65	1.92	1.24
Kevin Ryan	16	132	12.12%	53.49	-49.40	34.85	1.31	1.63
Nigel Tinkler	14	181	7.73%	48.06	-50.00	27.23	0.84	0.94

RIPON

Trainer	Wins	Runs	Strike Rate	% Rivals Beaten	P/L	Run To Form %	Impact Value	Market Value
Tim Easterby	65	508	12.80%	51.85	-70.96	34.84	1.08	1.13
David O'Meara	42	269	15.61%	56.35	7.42	39.86	1.32	1.35
Richard Fahey	40	281	14.23%	50.08	-42.36	31.92	1.16	1.27
Mark Johnston	27	219	12.33%	49.81	-80.53	38.46	0.82	1.32
William Haggas	18	54	33.33%	69.66	-11.39	56.54	2.18	2.61
Ruth Carr	15	107	14.02%	51.55	90.08	25.46	1.37	1.07
Nigel Tinkler	15	100	15.00%	51.51	9.08	29.00	1.39	1.01
Roger Varian	13	37	35.14%	69.36	0.70	56.76	2.61	2.63
Roger Fell	11	123	8.94%	50.78	-57.42	34.85	0.79	1.15
Michael Dods	11	76	14.47%	55.95	-8.47	42.16	1.29	1.12

SALISBURY

Trainer	Wins	Runs	Strike Rate	% Rivals Beaten	P/L	Run To Form %	Impact Value	Market Value
Richard Hannon	30	338	8.88%	51.97	-75.30	39.70	0.74	1.27
Andrew Balding	23	174	13.22%	51.23	-60.69	43.44	1.06	1.42
Ralph Beckett	21	142	14.79%	56.61	-27.55	39.35	1.22	1.46
Clive Cox	20	110	18.18%	61.65	0.42	49.71	1.59	1.47
Mick Channon	16	120	13.33%	50.69	-2.13	42.13	1.04	0.95
Rod Millman	16	156	10.26%	50.04	-71.72	28.28	0.89	1.09
Roger Varian	15	77	19.48%	64.31	-11.53	52.24	1.66	2.18
William Haggas	14	44	31.82%	69.57	18.12	62.77	2.85	2.50
Eve Johnson Houghton	12	99	12.12%	54.96	-33.78	37.56	1.02	1.19
Roger Charlton	12	64	18.75%	56.03	-11.50	48.09	1.54	1.61

SANDOWN PARK

Trainer	Wins	Runs	Strike Rate	% Rivals Beaten	P/L	Run To Form %	Impact Value	Market Value
Richard Hannon	30	233	12.88%	49.37	-17.56	41.39	1.10	1.09
John Gosden	25	126	19.84%	63.44	-43.73	58.54	1.61	2.14
Andrew Balding	22	177	12.43%	53.17	-23.41	46.10	1.02	1.28
Sir Michael Stoute	21	100	21.00%	57.79	-12.06	48.00	1.71	1.75
Charlie Appleby	21	78	26.92%	67.89	-11.63	65.27	2.03	2.25
William Haggas	18	84	21.43%	60.54	17.08	46.85	1.82	1.95
Clive Cox	17	119	14.29%	50.81	-28.06	37.33	1.19	1.27
David Menuisier	15	55	27.27%	63.63	32.65	67.39	2.50	1.37
Roger Charlton	12	72	16.67%	53.77	-6.93	42.26	1.31	1.43
Roger Varian	12	78	15.38%	58.71	-26.13	56.11	1.26	1.79

SOUTHWELL (AW)

Trainer	Wins	Runs	Strike Rate	% Rivals Beaten	P/L	Run To Form %	Impact Value	Market Value
Michael Appleby	97	769	12.61%	51.73	-253.42	29.38	1.02	1.32
K. R. Burke	49	252	19.44%	58.30	95.41	41.94	1.53	1.44
Richard Fahey	43	260	16.54%	55.20	-28.57	37.07	1.31	1.20
Scott Dixon	42	635	6.61%	49.22	-136.33	24.79	0.60	0.95
Ivan Furtado	34	251	13.55%	53.81	-10.99	31.58	1.23	1.23
Mark Johnston	33	141	23.40%	59.75	-13.90	40.55	1.72	1.62
Tony Carroll	31	216	14.35%	52.18	66.93	26.96	1.26	1.20
Tim Easterby	27	128	21.09%	54.69	80.96	33.59	1.87	1.27
David C. Griffiths	24	197	12.18%	50.46	-38.38	28.16	1.06	0.97
David Evans	24	214	11.21%	50.01	-26.38	25.96	0.95	1.16

THIRSK

Trainer	Wins	Runs	Strike Rate	% Rivals Beaten	P/L	Run To Form %	Impact Value	Market Value
Richard Fahey	38	287	13.24%	54.99	-30.77	33.08	1.38	1.34
Tim Easterby	35	427	8.20%	48.37	-134.90	27.79	0.88	1.06
David O'Meara	35	259	13.51%	58.56	14.64	34.86	1.38	1.48
Kevin Ryan	23	177	12.99%	54.87	-7.88	36.14	1.38	1.48
Michael Dods	20	248	8.06%	50.39	-96.15	31.87	0.88	1.24
William Haggas	17	45	37.78%	78.89	7.48	74.38	3.06	3.07
Paul Midgley	17	132	12.88%	49.89	1.25	23.58	1.47	1.18
John Quinn	12	114	10.53%	45.90	3.67	27.07	1.22	1.14
K. R. Burke	12	103	11.65%	56.23	-46.37	38.08	1.10	1.38
Declan Carroll	10	96	10.42%	53.90	-0.75	32.25	1.17	1.28

WETHERBY

Trainer	Wins	Runs	Strike Rate	% Rivals Beaten	P/L	Run To Form %	Impact Value	Market Value
Richard Fahey	7	30	23.33%	58.45	22.75	48.18	2.29	1.71
David O'Meara	6	32	18.75%	62.68	41.49	46.87	2.02	1.63
Roger Fell	4	23	17.39%	55.42	1.00	36.36	1.99	1.40
Tim Easterby	4	49	8.16%	55.18	-10.50	46.94	0.84	0.93
Declan Carroll	4	14	28.57%	71.25	21.00	50.00	3.10	1.52
John Gosden	4	9	44.44%	83.65	-0.21	50.00	4.89	4.41
William Haggas	3	10	30.00%	62.04	1.94	60.00	2.84	3.13
Ralph Beckett	3	5	60.00%	81.59	10.28	100.00	4.78	2.19
Jedd O'Keeffe	3	10	30.00%	68.14	8.00	40.00	3.41	1.58
David Barron	2	9	22.22%	53.22	7.00	22.22	2.63	1.53

WINDSOR

Trainer	Wins	Runs	Strike Rate	% Rivals Beaten	P/L	Run To Form %	Impact Value	Market Value
Richard Hannon	59	326	18.10%	59.52	14.56	44.46	1.52	1.61
Andrew Balding	28	151	18.54%	59.93	-13.24	48.43	1.56	1.65
Clive Cox	27	174	15.52%	58.11	-20.21	46.52	1.45	1.65
William Haggas	23	80	28.75%	68.60	-16.03	54.36	2.57	2.65
Mick Channon	22	152	14.47%	57.78	-25.76	38.15	1.33	1.37
Eve Johnson Houghton	22	142	15.49%	56.37	-18.33	44.19	1.44	1.41
Ed Walker	20	118	16.95%	61.86	-36.58	50.15	1.52	1.57
Ralph Beckett	19	122	15.57%	60.40	-8.50	51.26	1.34	1.62
Roger Varian	18	63	28.57%	69.35	1.84	61.19	2.57	2.42
Charles Hills	15	114	13.16%	52.84	-14.23	40.37	1.15	1.20

WOLVERHAMPTON (AW)

Trainer	Wins	Runs	Strike Rate	% Rivals Beaten	P/L	Run To Form %	Impact Value	Market Value
David Evans	76	688	11.05%	49.52	-92.62	32.59	1.03	1.10
Michael Appleby	66	637	10.36%	48.92	-129.83	32.34	0.94	1.14
Mark Johnston	62	505	12.28%	53.52	-133.20	47.21	1.03	1.39
Tony Carroll	59	577	10.23%	49.87	-84.21	32.92	1.01	1.16
Tom Dascombe	57	374	15.24%	59.56	68.84	48.22	1.34	1.55
David Loughnane	56	474	11.81%	52.40	11.31	37.71	1.13	1.18
Antony Brittain	53	518	10.23%	55.28	-93.07	36.63	0.99	1.09
Archie Watson	51	298	17.11%	57.32	-85.07	40.77	1.53	1.68
Richard Fahey	51	519	9.83%	52.93	-147.49	39.53	0.89	1.10
David O'Meara	51	464	10.99%	51.87	-53.68	33.91	1.01	1.14

YARMOUTH

Trainer	Wins	Runs	Strike Rate	% Rivals Beaten	P/L	Run To Form %	Impact Value	Market Value
William Haggas	36	153	23.53%	65.99	-19.33	54.97	1.85	2.17
John Gosden	33	94	35.11%	75.22	23.53	62.62	2.85	2.32
Chris Wall	26	132	19.70%	52.97	-23.78	41.07	1.67	1.50
David Simcock	25	135	18.52%	51.78	-10.38	44.94	1.30	1.29
Michael Bell	23	130	17.69%	52.65	-12.58	46.76	1.44	1.13
Roger Varian	23	118	19.49%	68.70	-26.48	58.60	1.58	1.88
Stuart Williams	22	176	12.50%	52.32	-71.50	38.42	0.95	1.14
Mark Johnston	20	138	14.49%	46.76	-40.85	43.48	0.96	1.21
Michael Appleby	18	205	8.78%	41.75	-58.47	27.24	0.72	0.92
Sir Mark Prescott Bt	16	53	30.19%	54.61	-11.09	50.94	2.22	1.40

YORK

Trainer	Wins	Runs	Strike Rate	% Rivals Beaten	P/L	Run To Form %	Impact Value	Market Value
Tim Easterby	39	451	8.65%	50.16	103.13	28.00	1.10	1.10
William Haggas	37	210	17.62%	59.42	-33.10	47.91	1.87	2.12
Richard Fahey	37	548	6.75%	50.31	-191.88	29.42	0.76	1.11
Mark Johnston	29	242	11.98%	47.17	13.76	31.30	1.23	1.21
John Gosden	24	85	28.24%	58.13	-3.12	56.03	2.24	2.13
David O'Meara	24	386	6.22%	49.32	-49.67	26.69	0.77	1.14
Michael Dods	23	149	15.44%	62.65	28.67	37.82	1.87	1.48
Andrew Balding	20	136	14.71%	55.55	70.95	47.79	1.43	1.30
Kevin Ryan	19	284	6.69%	48.57	-126.75	26.60	0.77	1.21
Richard Hannon	15	148	10.14%	54.56	2.40	37.24	1.15	1.38

INDEX

INDEX

Index To Photographers